DATE DUE

DE 17 '96	AP 23 '02		
MR 20 '97	JE 06 '02		
	NO 8 '02		
MY 27 '97	OC 2 '03		
	JE 1 '04		
AV 11 '97	AP 7 '05		
AU 11 '97	AG 6 '05		
MY 5 '98			
OC 22 '98			
MY 20 '99			
OC 25 '99			
DE 18 '99			
NO 2 '00			
OC 26 '01			
NO 16 '01			

DEMCO 38-296

Intimate
Betrayal

Intimate Betrayal

Understanding and Responding to the Trauma of Acquaintance Rape

Vernon R. Wiehe
Ann L. Richards

SAGE Publications
International Educational and Professional Publisher
Thousand Oaks   London   New Delhi

2455 Teller Road
Thousand Oaks, California 91320
E-mail: order@sagepub.com

SAGE Publications Ltd.
6 Bonhill Street
London EC2A 4PU
United Kingdom

SAGE Publications India Pvt. Ltd.
M-32 Market
Greater Kailash I
New Delhi 110 048 India

Printed in the United States of America

Library of Congress Cataloging-in-Publication Data

Wiehe, Vernon R.
  Intimate betrayal : Understanding and responding to the trauma of
acquaintance rape / by Vernon R. Wiehe, Ann L. Richards.
    p. cm.
  Includes bibliographical references and index.
  ISBN 0-8039-7360-8 (cl.). — ISBN 0-8039-7361-6 (pbk.).
  1. Acquaintance rape—United States. I. Richards, Ann L.
II. Title.
HV6561.W53 1995
362.88'3—dc20   95-4377

This book is printed on acid-free paper.

95 96 97 98 99 10 9 8 7 6 5 4 3 2 1

Sage Production Editor: Tricia K. Bennett
Typesetter: Janelle LeMaster

Contents

Rape is a crime against sleep and memory; its afterimage imprints itself like an irreversible negative from the camera obscura of dreams. Throughout our lives these three dead and slaughtered men would teach us over and over of the abidingness, the terrible constancy, that accompanies a wound to the spirit. Though our bodies would heal, our souls had sustained a damage beyond compensation. Violence sends deep roots into the heart, it has no seasons; it is always ripe, evergreen.

It can happen to anyone, but it damn sure shouldn't.
—An acquaintance rape survivor

Preface

The title we have chosen for this book, *Intimate Betrayal*, graphically portrays the nature of acquaintance rape and its effect on the victim. To be *intimate* with someone implies a close and personal relationship. A sense of trust undergirds such a relationship. *Betrayal*, on the other hand, implies treachery, fraud, deception—a violation of this trust. The two words, when put together, represent an oxymoron or the pointedly foolish because the words, in a sense, are contradictory or incongruous (Follett, 1966). Yet, that is the nature of acquaintance rape. An acquaintance—a friend, date, family member, neighbor, employer—someone known, someone trusted, violently violates that relationship. The victim is intimately betrayed.

The Subject

Acquaintance rape is a serious social problem in American society. A need exists for information and education about acquaintance rape. Although most individuals have some knowledge of rape, the concept generally is thought of in terms of rape by a stranger. The subject of rape by an acquaintance is less well-known. Also, stranger and acquaintance rape are perceived differently by the general public and sometimes even by those who work with survivors and perpetrators. Research shows, for example, that individuals are more tolerant of acquaintance rape compared to stranger rape (Johnson & Jackson, 1988; Quackenbush, 1989). A greater tendency exists to identify with the victim of a stranger rape and the violence, stealth, and shock of this situation compared to a victim raped by an acquaintance. Victims of acquaintance rape are likely to be blamed for their assault, especially if there has been any degree of intimacy between the assailant and victim prior to the rape. Obviously, the way in which acquaintance rape is perceived or understood by others affects what victims do following their assault, the services they receive, the prosecution of perpetrators, and efforts to prevent the problem.

Acquaintance rape is a timely subject. Individuals are postponing marriage until later and consequently are dating longer or are living together. Thus, the lengthening of the dating or nonmarital state allows for greater opportunity for acquaintance rape to occur, especially in the context of the courtship relationship. The subject also is important and timely because abuse in the dating relationship may be a precursor of what will occur in the marital relationship. As efforts are made to prosecute offenders and prevent acquaintance rape, perhaps this can also affect abuse that occurs in the marital relationship.

The Audience

We had a specific audience and purpose in mind when we combined our interests and efforts in writing this book—a university researcher, and a psychotherapist and former associate director of a women's center. The specific audience to which the book is directed is individuals who work with victims of acquaintance rape or who work with persons at risk of becoming a victim or perpetrator. These would include the following:

- Personnel directors
- Clergy
- Teachers

- School guidance counselors
- Personnel employed by college and university dean of students' offices
- Persons working in the criminal justice system
- Individuals employed in family counseling agencies and community mental health centers
- Rape crisis counselors

The purpose of this book is to inform and to educate about the nature, scope, and impact of acquaintance rape on its victims, how to intervene with those who have experienced the problem, and ways acquaintance rape can be prevented. We are aware that some individuals who may come in contact with acquaintance rape victims or potential victims and perpetrators may not be trained in the helping professions. For that reason, especially in Chapter 9, the chapter on recovery, we have erred in the direction of being very basic in our approach on how to help survivors in their recovery from the trauma of their sexual assault. In the chapter on recovery, we discuss basic issues relative to the helping relationship, such as forming a relationship, confidentiality, and making a referral. We feel the nature of these issues is somewhat different when helping acquaintance rape survivors and thus even seasoned counselors can profit from a review of these basic issues in the context of acquaintance rape. A friend who at one time was employed in a rape crisis center affirmed our purpose for writing the book and the audience to whom we directed the book. After reading the manuscript, she commented, "This is the kind of book I needed when I was working with acquaintance rape victims."

Although the book is not directed specifically to individuals who have experienced acquaintance rape, we are certain some survivors will read it. If you are an acquaintance rape survivor, we hope this book will help you realize that you are not alone in the betrayal you have experienced and be motivated to seek help and to begin your healing process.

Who better can educate and inform others about the problem of acquaintance rape than those who have experienced the problem. For that reason, comments of the women who participated in our research are used throughout the book. These survivors describe in their own words their intimate betrayal and its impact on their lives. Hopefully, their comments will provide you an opportunity to experience with a varied group of survivors what they uniquely experienced as well as what they hold in common with other survivors. We have incorporated with the survivors' comments the professional literature on acquaintance rape, enabling you to put these comments into a theoretical framework for understanding this social problem.

The Research

This book reports the findings of a research project in which 278 women participated who had experienced sexual assault from an acquaintance. Of these women, 40 were raped by their husbands. The data on this subsample is reported in a separate chapter on marital rape. Copies of the research questionnaire (see Appendix) were sent to rape crisis centers throughout the United States asking center directors to give the questionnaire to women who had been raped by an acquaintance. Individuals responded voluntarily and anonymously in prepaid envelopes addressed to the researchers. Postmarks on envelopes in which respondents returned their questionnaires revealed they came from all but 5 of the 50 states (Indiana, Delaware, Rhode Island, Alabama, Maryland). The data were collected over a 2-year period.

Statistical data have been used sparingly throughout the book. Rather, the responses have been analyzed qualitatively emphasizing the survivors' thoughts and comments. Qualitative analysis was used so that you can feel and understand how the survivors experienced their rape, the ways this trauma has affected their lives, and their thoughts on how the problem of acquaintance rape can be prevented. Although it was not possible to include the comments of all respondents, a deliberate effort was made to avoid sensationalism when selecting the survivors' comments to illustrate the major themes. The comments are reproduced with only limited editing to correct grammar.

Format of the Book

The first chapter of the book will introduce you to the problem of acquaintance rape and define the key terms. Subsequent chapters will focus on the research participants (Chapter 2), the assault (Chapter 3), the survivors' response to the assault (Chapter 4), and its impact on their lives (Chapter 5). Chapter 6 discusses marital rape, a form of acquaintance rape, and reports data on a subsample of 40 women raped by their husbands. Chapter 7 presents theoretical frameworks for understanding this social problem. Legal aspects of acquaintance rape is the theme of Chapter 8. Chapters 9 and 10 focus on the recovery process from the perspectives of the therapist and the survivor. Chapter 11 emphasizes acquaintance rape prevention. Finally, the Appendix includes a copy of the research instrument and materials that you can use as you engage in educational efforts toward the prevention of acquaintance rape.

We are aware that numerous staff members working in rape crisis centers throughout the country used the research questionnaire as a means of facilitating survivors to think about their rape by having them answer the questionnaire and then discussing their responses in individual therapy sessions, group therapy sessions, or both. The research questionnaire is reproduced in the Appendix of the book for those who may wish to use it in a similar manner.

Word of Thanks

First, we want to thank the authors who contributed two chapters to this book based on their expertise. Chapter 6 on marital rape was written by Patricia Lynn Peacock, a doctoral student at the University of Tennessee. Dr. Gary Paquin, an attorney and social worker, wrote Chapter 8 titled "The Legal Aspects of Acquaintance Rape."

Our appreciation is extended to the many individuals who in some way contributed to the preparation of this book: Lisa Stofer, formerly Assistant Dean of Students for Health Education at the University of Kentucky, who shared her knowledge and expertise in acquaintance rape prevention; Tony Mazzaro, Associate Professor of Social Work at Northern Kentucky University, and Dr. Karl

Stukenberg, clinical psychologist, formerly at Northern Kentucky University and now Assistant Professor at Xavier University, who brought their clinical experience to their review of the material on recovery and provided helpful comments; Sherri Chapin, ministerial candidate with the United Methodist Church and Deanna Welsh, former sexual assault counselor with the Women's Crisis Center of Northern Kentucky and currently MSW candidate, who thoughtfully and thoroughly read the manuscript and gave us the practitioner's point of view; Steve Richards, who patiently provided technical assistance to his otherwise computer-deficient mother; and spouses and colleagues who gave ongoing support and encouragement to our efforts.

Numerous personal notes were attached to the research questionnaires. Many of these notes expressed interest in the results of the research, but others were notes of appreciation to the researchers for their interest in this subject. Following are two such comments:

> You don't know how helpful this was to me to complete the questionnaire. In some respects I feel a burden has been lifted.

> I am so glad that someone cares enough for those of us that have been through events tragic enough to prevent a normal life, to try to compile this information to help others. Thank you.

We want to express our appreciation to the directors of rape crisis centers who gave the research questionnaire to women in their agencies who had sought help for their victimization by an acquaintance. Our thanks especially to the 278 women who shared with us their painful and bitter experiences of a sexual assault by an acquaintance. It is our hope that their responses to the questionnaire that formed the basis of this book will help mental health professionals in their recovery work with acquaintance rape survivors and in their efforts in preventing this problem.

—Vernon R. Wiehe
—Ann L. Richards

References

Follett, W. (1966). *Modern American usage*. New York: Hill & Wang.

Johnson, J. D., & Jackson, L. A., Jr. (1988). Assessing the effects of factors that might underlie the differential perception of acquaintance and stranger rape. *Sex Roles, 19,* 37-45.

Quackenbush, R. L. (1989). A comparison of androgynous, masculine sex-typed and undifferentiated males on dimensions of attitudes toward rape. *Journal of Research in Personality, 23,* 318-342.

It is always the one that you never sus-
pected who is the perpetrator.
　　　　　—An acquaintance rape survivor

1　The Problem

I had dated Ted for several months. We met through some mutual
friends. I really liked him. He was good-looking and a really neat guy.
One evening after going out together for dinner, he invited me to his
apartment to listen to some tapes of a band we had talked about at
dinner.

　　As we sat on the couch and listened to the music, he became very
aggressive. We had "made out" before but never anything really
heavy—mainly hugging and kissing. When he started putting his
hands in places I didn't appreciate, I told him so. He acted as if this
was a challenge and continued to do what he had been doing. At one
point I got up to leave. He pushed me into the bedroom, threw me
down on the bed, and raped me. When it was over, I was crying and
hurting. His only reply was, "You know you liked it."

My girlfriend invited me to a party her boyfriend's fraternity was
having at his frat house. Although I didn't attend that school, I
thought it might be a good way to meet some new friends. There
were lots of people at the party.

　　I met a guy who had worked for the same company I worked for
during the past summer but at a different store. We seemed to really
hit it off together. He invited me to a poolroom in the basement of the
frat house to shoot some pool. I noticed he started talking dirty while
there but I ignored it since he had been drinking quite a bit of beer. He

1

had shut the door when we went into the poolroom. We were the only ones in the room. At one time I was leaning over the table to set up a shot. I felt him pushing at me from behind. After I took the shot, I looked back over my shoulder. He had his erect penis in his hand and was pushing against me. He told me to perform oral sex on him. When I refused, he grabbed my hair, pushed me down, and forced me to do it. I was too frightened to scream. I immediately left the party. I was later told by a friend that it wouldn't have mattered if I had screamed because a closed door in the frat house meant no one was to bother anyone inside the room.

I had worked at this store about two months. My boss, who was old enough to be my father, often made suggestive remarks about women who came into the store. I never thought much about it. I figured all men did this because I had heard men at other places where I had worked talk this way. When we were cleaning up the store one night after closing hours, he "goosed" me with a broom handle. I laughed it off not thinking that much about it. Soon after that he grabbed me from the back between my legs attempting to fondle me. I was scared as to what he might do next. I quickly finished my work and left. I never went back to work there. He sent me my check through the mail. I didn't feel I could say anything because he owned the store.
     I never thought about this as rape until later I saw a TV program on sexual assault sponsored by the rape crisis center in the city where I live. This started me thinking about the terrible fear I have of men that I developed after this incident. I contacted the center and joined a support group that really has been helpful.

Although generally I enjoy making love to my husband, there are times when I'm upset over an argument we've had, or I've just had a hard day at work and with the kids, and I don't want to have sex.
     If my husband wants sex, he says he is going to get it. It's like he feels it's his right. When he acts this way, and I don't really participate like he feels I should, then he's angry and I'm really in trouble. He says things like he is going out and find a woman who wants it. I feel terrible then. When he forces me to have sex when I don't want it, I feel like I've been raped.

These are not quotations from the script of a play or from a novel. These are comments from women who are survivors of acquaintance rape. Acquaintance rape is a social problem in American society that is slowly gaining recognition for what it is—namely, a violation of power between the sexes. Acquaintance rape is not merely an act of sex. It is sex fused with and degraded by intimidation, domination, and, in some cases, bodily harm.

Definition of Terms

Everyone is familiar with the term *rape*. The word creates frightening feelings. It implies violence, power, and force. The word also conjures up in one's mind a scene involving stealth, secrecy, and an attack. This can be felt in the following account of a young female executive who was a victim of stranger rape:

> I was leaving my office and had just entered the parking garage. There were only a few cars remaining in the garage because I had worked late in my office to finish a report from my boss. As I was approaching my car, a man jumped out from behind one of the large concrete pillars in the garage. He pinned my arms behind my back, threatened to kill me with a knife that he pressed against my throat, threw me to the concrete floor, and raped me.

Acquaintance

The young woman in the above account is unwarily attacked by a stranger in her office parking garage. The assailant is someone unknown to the victim, a stranger. Acquaintance rape is similar in some ways to this young woman's account of her sexual assault, but in some ways it is very different. The horror of the assault remains the same. Its impact on the victim is similar in terms of the violation of the victim's privacy and dignity and the devastation of her sense of well-being. However, the context in which the assault occurs and the relationship of the two parties differ between stranger and acquaintance rape.

In acquaintance rape, the attack occurs not in the abrupt context of a stranger—someone unknown to the victim—suddenly appearing and assaulting the victim. Rather, the victim and perpetrator know each other; they are acquaintances, as the four vignettes reported earlier indicate. The acquaintance in these sexual assaults may be someone the victim is dating, a high school or college classmate who sits near the victim in class, or someone the victim meets or sees on an occasional basis at fraternity and sorority parties. The acquaintance may be a fellow employee in the company where both work, or he may even be her boss. The acquaintance may also be a family member, for example, a brother-in-law who rapes his brother's wife. In some instances, the acquaintance is a spouse.

In summary, the term *acquaintance* will be used in this book to refer to a sexual assault that occurs between two individuals who are acquainted with one another or are known to each other. Included in the term will be individuals who are dating, often referred to in the literature as *date rape*. The term also will include individuals sexually assaulted by someone who is a friend, employer, or just someone the victim knows, such as an apartment manager. Also, to be included in the term acquaintance are individuals who were sexually assaulted by their spouse, generally referred to in the literature as *marital rape*. Chapter 6 will focus specifically on a subsample of 40 women who were survivors of marital rape—namely, rape by their marital partner. (Although this book will focus primarily on sexual assaults in heterosexual relationships, this social problem also occurs in homosexual relationships.)

Although different terms are now being used for different types of rape—stranger rape, acquaintance rape, date rape, marital rape—unfortunately, in some instances, the public media have used these terms to distinguish the severity of the crime. Thus, stranger rape may be presented as the most serious type of rape and acquaintance or marital rape as the least serious or injurious because the perpetrator and victim knew each other or were married to each other. A basic premise of this book, as reflected in the survivors' comments in the following chapters, is that rape is rape whether committed by a stranger, employer, friend, date, or spouse. Rape must be defined by the act itself; from a legal point of view, its seriousness must be judged in relation to the extent of injury that occurred or whether or not a deadly weapon was used rather than in terms of the relationship of the perpetrator and victim. Contrary to popular notion, the impact of a rape from a perpetrator known and trusted by the victim may even be greater than sexual assault from a total stranger (Troop, 1992).

Rape

For the purposes of the research on which this book is based, *rape* is defined as any sexual activity that one experiences without giving consent. This includes fondling, oral, anal, and vaginal intercourse or other unwanted sexual activity. Sexually assaultive behaviors occurring between acquaintances is often conceptualized along a continuum according to the degree of force or coercion involved. Extreme positions on such a continuum might range from unwanted touching, at times referred to in the literature as sexual imposition, to the most extreme form of sexual assault—that is, rape.

The definition of rape to be used in this book, however, is broader than the way the term is generally defined. The legal definition of rape focuses on forceful intercourse—namely, penile-vaginal sexual intercourse. The broader definition that will be used in this book, consistent with feminist thought, includes any unwanted sexual activity (Russell, 1986). If both parties do not consent to the sexual activity, then the act becomes a violation of the privacy and dignity of the individual who is the target or victim of the behavior, even if the perpetrator and victim know each other. The act becomes rape.

Of the 276 participants in the research, 229 (82%) were forced against their wishes to have sexual intercourse with their assailant. The remainder were forced to engage in other sexual acts against their wishes. Table 1.1 reports the sexual behaviors in which survivors were forced to engage.

Survivor or Victim

The term *survivor* rather than *victim* generally will be used to refer to individuals who have been raped by an acquaintance. Survivor is a preferable name to give individuals who have been traumatized by sexual abuse. A survivor is one who has experienced a trauma and lives to tell about it. The term survivor implies that the victim has succeeded or endured, despite experiencing a serious trauma.

TABLE 1.1 Unwanted Sexual Behaviors That Survivors Were Forced to Engage In

Behavior	Percentage [a]	(n)
Intercourse	82	(229)
Perpetrator fondling victim	64	(177)
Victim being forced to fondle perpetrator	35	(96)
Victim being forced to fellate perpetrator	32	(89)
Perpetrator fellating victim	25	(70)
Perpetrator engaging victim in anal sex	18	(49)

a. Percentages do not total 100% because survivors identified more than one behavior.

The term victim, on the other hand, implies helplessness. A victim of an automobile accident, for example, may be trapped in the car or may even be unconscious. The accounts of those participating in this research certainly depict a spirit of survivorship despite the rape's impact on their personal lives.

At times, however, victim may be used interchangeably with survivor. This will occur especially when reference is being made to the person at the time the rape occurs. This is not meant to imply that the individual will not become a survivor of this trauma.

Perpetrator

The term *perpetrator* will be used synonomously with the terms *assailant* or *offender*, referring to the individual who committed the rape. Because the book focuses entirely on acquaintance rape by male perpetrators, masculine pronouns will be used to refer to the perpetrator.

Nature and Scope of the Problem

How prevalent is acquaintance rape? How frequently does this problem occur? Unfortunately, statistical data reporting the number of arrests by local police departments aggregated on a national basis, known as the *Uniform Crime Reports*, compiled annually by the U.S. Department of Justice, do not distinguish between stranger and acquaintance rapes. The National Crime Victimization Survey, a survey by interviewers of a large number of households in the United States, also compiled and printed annually by the U.S. Department of Justice, does distinguish between stranger and nonstranger rapes but uses a very narrow definition of rape compared to the broader definition being used in this book. However, based on this narrow definition of rape ("carnal knowledge through the use of force or the threat of force, including attempts"), several comparisons are made of stranger and nonstranger rapes that help us understand the nature of acquaintance rape. Nonstranger rapes usually occurred in the victim's home (48%) or in or near a friend's home (24%). Nonstranger compared to stranger rapes did not involve the use of a weapon. Victims of nonstranger rape did not differ from their counterparts raped by strangers in their efforts to protect themselves from their assailant, including verbal persuasion, physical force, or attempting to flee. Generally, nonstranger rapes involved only one offender. The ages of offenders did not differ significantly between stranger and nonstranger rapes. About three fourths of each type were committed by men over 20 years of age. Rapes committed by nonstrangers were less likely to be reported to the police as compared to stranger rapes. The reason most frequently cited by victims for not reporting the assault was that the rape was a personal or private matter. Other reasons cited were the fear of reprisal (22%) and the victim's belief that the police would be inefficient, ineffective, or insensitive (U.S. Department of Justice, 1991).

Whenever data on the number of acquaintance rapes are reported, several factors must be kept in mind. Statistical data on acquaintance rape reflect only the tip of the iceberg for the number of rapes actually occurring, because underreporting is believed to be the norm. Several reasons may be cited for this, including victim self-blame for the assault, embarrassment related to the reaction of friends and family members, fear of reprisal from the assailant, and the failure of the victim to identify her assault as rape. Relative to the latter factor, in a study involving 234 women who were raped by an acquaintance, 61% (143) of the women did not consider their experience as rape at the time it happened. Fifty-eight stated they had never even heard of the concept of acquaintance rape before it happened to them (Koss, Dinero, Seibel, & Cox, 1988). Thus, based on limited reporting, it is nearly impossible to determine the exact extent of this problem. Estimates indicate that the number of reported rapes, both stranger and acquaintance rapes, represent from 10% to 50% of the actual number of rapes occurring (Koss, 1985).

Summary

This chapter has introduced you to the problem of acquaintance rape by presenting some case vignettes, terms to be used throughout the book in discussing the subject, and statistical information on the nature and scope of the problem.

You can't tell bad guys by looking at them.

—An acquaintance rape survivor

2 The Victim and the Perpetrator

The two key figures in an acquaintance rape are the victim and the perpetrator. Who are these individuals? How did they meet? This chapter will introduce you to them. Statistical information provided by the respondents will be presented. More important, comments made by the victims will be shared with you so that you can become acquainted with these individuals. Hopefully, with this information you will develop an understanding of acquaintance rape and will be better able to help survivors in their recovery from the trauma they have experienced.

The Victim

The average age of the survivors at the time they completed the research questionnaire was 30 years compared to their age at the time they were sexually assaulted, which was 22 years. Thus, for many of the survivors, time had lapsed between when they were raped and when they were involved in their healing process and completed the research instrument. You will recall that the research data were collected through rape crisis centers where survivors later sought help for their sexual victimization. The average age of the perpetrator at the time of the assault was 25 years. Based on this information we can conclude that both the victim and perpetrator were in their young adult years—the courtship years—a high-risk time for acquaintance rape.

Of the 234 survivors, 80% (186) sexually assaulted by an acquaintance were Caucasian, 14% (32) were African American, and the remaining 6% (16) were of other racial and ethnic backgrounds.

On the average, survivors at the time of their assault by an acquaintance were attending college or had completed one year of specialized training. At the time of their rape, 34% (78) had completed high school or less; 66% were attending college, had completed college, or had done graduate work. At the time the survivors participated in this research, their educational status had changed to the following: 20% (45) had completed high school or less compared to 80% who were attending college, had completed college, or had done graduate work. Thus, many of the survivors continued their education following their rape and were college educated at the time they participated in the research.

How Did They Meet?

Respondents to the research were asked the nature of their relationship to the perpetrator and how they met. Table 2.1 reports the relationship of the perpetrators and their victims.

Most survivors, 50% (117), described their perpetrator as a friend. A total of 10% (25) of the rapes involved a work situation where the perpetrator was a coworker or the victim's boss, and 3% (7) were customers the victim served.

Although these statistics are important in understanding the relationship of the perpetrator and victim, they fail to report the emotional context of the relationship in which the assault occurred. For this information we will turn to specific comments of survivors as they describe their relationship to the perpetrator. The comments will be organized according to the major categories found in Table 2.1.

TABLE 2.1 Relationship of Perpetrators and Victims

Relationship	Percentage	(n)
Friend	50	(117)
Fellow student	18	(41)
Boyfriend or ex-boyfriend	12	(29)
Coworker or boss	10	(25)
Neighbor	4	(9)
Customer	3	(7)
Other	3	(8)
Total	100	(236)

NOTE: As will occur in subsequent tables, the 40 individuals raped by their spouse are not included in these analyses.

Friend

The largest percentage of perpetrators were friends or acquaintances of the victim. You will find that the relationship of the victim and perpetrator at the time of the assault was no different from relationships in which each of us are involved on a daily basis.

> I met him in a store where I was buying some jeans. He joked with me about the small size I needed and we became involved in conversation. He asked me out.

> He was a friend of the family—my Dad's best buddy. I have known him all of my life.

> I met him at a party. He was a college student at a high school party. He introduced himself to me and several of my friends.

> I met him at an outdoor party. He came over by my friend and me and introduced himself. We visited for several hours and he invited me to breakfast. He was a perfect gentleman. I was impressed by his openness.

> I have known him since infancy. We grew up together in the same neighborhood and went all the way through elementary and high school together. Our parents also were friends.

He was my husband's best friend and his family was friends of our family for years.

I met him at an outpatient treatment program for alcoholism. We shared this common problem and became friends because we could talk to one another about this and things we held in common. For example, we were both about the same age; both of us had been married before. We were friends for almost a year before he raped me. We did not date but spent time together as friends.

Fellow Student

The perpetrator in 18% (41) of the situations was a fellow student or classmate in high school or most often in college.

I met him in an English class at Oregon State University. He had recently returned from Vietnam and was a student on the GI Bill. He was handsome, charming, and flirtatious.

We met at college. He was a star football player—BMOC (Big Man on Campus). I was a freshman volleyball player. Everyone thought he was very good-looking. I was honored when he asked me out.

We were both active in our respective sorority and fraternity. We saw each other frequently at "Greek" parties and also in many classes.

Boyfriend or Ex-Boyfriend

Respondents reported their assailant was someone they knew well through a dating relationship.

We had gone to the same high school. He had already graduated when I started dating him. He had previously dated one of my friends. I ran into him one evening. We went out and had a few beers. We started seeing each other.

He was a steady boyfriend. We had met in high school.

We originally met at a coffee shop at which I worked. He regularly came to the shop for coffee. One evening he asked me out on a date and I accepted. We eventually became boyfriend and girlfriend.

I originally met my boyfriend at a singles dance for the 30+ age group. This was a group primarily for professionals.

Coworker or Boss

For some of the victims, the assailant was a fellow employee or their employer.

I was working as a secretary in a university setting. The perpetrator was a graduate student who occasionally helped out in my office.

We worked together. We became good friends on the job.

I was staying at the "Reverend's" house on a short-term basis as a live-in nanny. The "Reverend" was the perpetrator.

The perpetrator was my employer. I responded to an ad in the newspaper for the job. Also, the job had been listed with the Office of Career Development at the university I attended.

I was working at a convenience store—part of a chain of stores. He was manager of another store across town. We were introduced through a mutual supervisor.

He was my first sergeant in the military (Air Force).

I met him at a national park where we both worked. He was a seasonal park ranger; I was a seasonal park naturalist. We became acquainted, hiked together, and visited with each other from time to time.

Neighbor

A neighbor, often someone who lived in the same apartment complex and whom the victim knew, became an assailant.

He lived in my apartment complex. We met on several occasions in the parking lot and talked. We became friends.

I met him by the swimming pool in my apartment complex. We started talking.

TABLE 2.2 How Well Did the Victim Know the Perpetrator?

Extent	Percentage	(n)
Knew perpetrator well	41	(97)
Knew perpetrator somewhat well	29	(68)
Did not know perpetrator well	30	(71)
Total	100	(236)

Customer

For a few victims, a customer in the store where they worked was the perpetrator of a sexual assault.

He was a regular customer in the store where I worked and we became friends. I was going through a bad divorce, and he seemed interested and concerned. I thought he was someone I could rely on, someone I could trust in the light of the horrible marriage I had just left.

Knowledge of the Perpetrator

The research participants were asked how long and how well they knew the perpetrator. The average amount of time most survivors knew the perpetrator at the time their assault occurred was 6 months to a year. Thus, in most instances the relationship was relatively new; however, the perpetrator and victim were certainly not strangers.

A 5-point Likert type scale was used to collect data on how well the perpetrator and victim knew each other. The findings were collapsed into three major categories as reported in Table 2.2. Nearly two thirds of the respondents knew their assailant *somewhat well* or *well*. These data may be influenced by the fact that the rape occurred during past years and many of the survivors were involved in individual counseling or were members of support groups for rape victims. Thus, as they look back on their assault, they now may conclude that they did not know their assailant very well even though at the time they may have felt closer to the perpetrator.

Summary

Statistical data on the nature of the relationship of the perpetrators and survivors, and especially the descriptions by the survivors of their relationship to their assailant, give the impression of the harmless nature of this relationship prior to the sexual assault. The relationship between the victim and the assailant was no different from the multitude of relationships each of us moves in and out of on a daily basis—a family friend, fellow student, boyfriend, co-worker or boss, neighbor, or a customer where we work. Apart from perhaps the relationship of boyfriend and girlfriend, nothing sexual is implied in any of these relationships. Even in the dating relationship sex on demand is certainly not implied. However, as we shall see in the next chapter, these relationships were turned into a sexual relationship overshadowed by violence, dominance, and power.

It can happen to anyone.
—An acquaintance rape survivor

3 The Assault

In this chapter, we will study the circumstances surrounding the rape. Survivors will share information on where the rape by an acquaintance occurred. The survivors will discuss factors in their relationship with their perpetrators as they looked back on what happened that made them uncomfortable—but at the time they ignored. The use of drugs and alcohol by the perpetrator and survivor will also be reported from the research data.

The Setting

Where did the rape by an acquaintance occur? Table 3.1 presents an analysis of survivors' responses to this question.

The largest percentage (58%) of the attacks occurred in familiar surroundings to the victim—namely, in her residence, the perpetrator's residence, or in a friend's apartment or home. What should have been a safe place for two people to spend time together turned into a setting for a sexual assault.

Criticism is often made of acquaintance rape victims who invite a friend to their apartment or who go to a friend's apartment and

TABLE 3.1 Where the Rape Occurred

Place	Percentage	(n)
Victim's apartment or home	29	(69)
Perpetrator's apartment or home	24	(56)
Friend's apartment or home	5	(11)
Motel	2	(6)
At place of employment	4	(9)
Secluded area, public park	5	(12)
Car, boat	17	(40)
Dormitory or fraternity house	3	(6)
Other	11	(27)
Total	100	(236)

then are sexually assaulted. The assumption appears to be made by some men that an invitation to a date or friend's apartment, or a woman accepting an invitation to their apartment implies that sexual activity will occur. How often doesn't one hear in jokes the phrase, "Your home or mine?" The statement evokes laughter based on an underlying but false assumption—namely, that sex is going to occur and a decision must be made where it will take place.

Research shows that many men accept this assumption, especially men who hold traditional or stereotypical views of male/female relationships. For example, in studies where male and female students viewed scenarios of two individuals going out on a date, who initiated the date, who paid, or where the couple went were interpreted by men as cues indicative of how much the woman wanted sex. For example, if the woman asked the man out, allowed him to pay the dating expenses, and went to his apartment, this was regarded by some men as a "sex-willingness" cue. If the man was correct in this perception, there was no problem. However, if he misread her cues, he may interpret this as having been "led on" by her. For some men, feeling they have been led on, increases their justifiability for rape (Muehlenhard, 1988; Muehlenhard, Friedman, & Thomas, 1985).

Public opinion reflects agreement with the assumption that if a woman goes to a man's apartment or invites him to her residence, then she is to blame if sexual activity that she does not desire occurs. This can be seen in the way the general public blames the victim for having invited the acquaintance to her apartment or for accepting an invitation to his residence. Many persons would probably blame the following survivor for what happened to her after inviting a date to her apartment:

> At dinner I learned he had brought a cassette tape for me to hear. I suggested going back to my apartment to hear it because my apartment was only two blocks away from the restaurant.

Allowing someone into your apartment can extend beyond the dating relationship and may involve a salesman or repairman. Undoubtedly, a quick appraisal is made by the woman regarding the safety of a situation before inviting a salesman or repairman into her home. The element of trust in the other person is involved when a woman admits the person into her house. In acquaintance rape this trust is violated and the scene becomes a setting for sexual assault. A survivor, raped by her neighbor whom she knew and who also worked as the maintenance man in the apartment complex where she lived, describes what happened to her:

> I admitted him to my apartment even though it was late. He said the landlord had told him to repair my leaking faucet. He said he had to fix it at that time because he was going away the next day. But after he was in my apartment, he started telling me about his distrust and anger at his wife, and then speculating about sex with me. I felt I should not have let him come in, that I should have been able to make him leave. I felt I was to blame because I was stupid and let him come in.
>   He had a utility belt on with tools (pliers, screwdriver, and so forth). I did not want to make him angry at me, but I tried to talk him out of the assault and told him to keep his hands off me. My 18-month-old daughter was in the room. I did not want to scare her by yelling and fighting. Nor did I want him to kill me and be alone with her. I was intimidated by him, vulnerable because of my child.

Another survivor vividly describes her assault by a neighbor whom she attempted to befriend:

It was 3:00 a.m. in the morning. I was asleep in my mobile home
where I lived. It's a quiet neighborhood. My father purchased this
home for me and went to a great deal of effort to make sure I was in
the safest part of the mobile home park. (We live in a community
where there is a large Navy base and my father didn't want me by
any of those Navy boys because he was afraid of what might happen.
So, I was carefully put in the best part of the park.)

There was a knock on my door. I answered it and found it was my
next door neighbor's son who is 16 years old. He told me his Mom
and Dad had come home drunk and had kicked him out of the house.
He needed a place to stay. Being from a small town, I was raised to
help my neighbors. I had a hide-a-bed couch that I made into a bed
for him and I went back to bed. I had to work the next morning so I
went right to sleep. About 3:30 a.m. I awoke to find him in my bed.
He told me he had a knife and I had better turn the light on. I did.
Next he told me to take all my clothes off. I did. He performed oral
sex on me and made me do the same. Then he raped me.

A survivor tells what happened to her:

We met at the restaurant where I was working as a waitress. He
had stopped by my workplace several times to see me and finally
asked me for a date. He was a typical, nice guy, good-looking, well-
mannered, and sweet. (I was, too.) He wanted to go to his apartment,
which was in his parent's home. I agreed. Later in the evening, he
sexually assaulted me.

The following comment is from a young woman who had known
her assailant for approximately a year. Her assailant had formerly
dated a close friend of hers. She reports:

We were walking in a wooded area together. He directed me into a
less-lighted path and pretended there was something dangerous so
I would walk closer to him. That is where I was raped.

A Retrospective View

There is a popular saying that "hindsight is better than foresight."
All of us can look back on an event and regret that we didn't take

another course of action. There is no value, however, in using information gained from retrospection to blame ourselves for what happened. In many instances, the knowledge was not available to us at the time or our awareness of what was happening at the time was only sharpened after the occurrence of the event. However, the information gained from looking back may provide us clues for preventing the event from occurring again.

Sometimes women who are raped can look back and recognize behavior by the perpetrator that made them uncomfortable before the rape occurred. Participants in the research were asked to recall any such behaviors or attitudes. The purpose of gathering this information was not to blame the survivor for having failed to recognize these warning signs, but to share with others this information with the hope of preventing situations that may lead to a sexual assault.

Substance Abuse

An analysis of the participants' responses revealed several significant themes. Many respondents expressed concern about the perpetrator's use of alcohol or drugs, both at the time the assault occurred as well as earlier during the period of their acquaintance. According to the survivors, of the 236 perpetrators, 60% (142) were using alcohol or drugs at the time of their assault, 34% (79) were not using any such substance, and it was unknown to the survivors if the remaining 6% (15) were under the influence of alcohol or drugs. Respondents reported that the perpetrator's use of alcohol or drugs appeared to increase their aggressiveness and interfered with their attempts to dissuade the perpetrator when the latter's behavior was out of line. Only 37% (86) of the survivors indicated they were using alcohol or drugs at the time of the assault.

The use of drugs and alcohol in acquaintance rape situations will be discussed more fully in Chapter 7, which focuses on understanding acquaintance rape. However, at this time we should mention that alcohol and drugs can serve as a disinhibitor for men in their ability to control aggression and for women in their attempts to resist assault.

Offender Attitudes and Behavior

The survivors identified additional attitudes and behaviors that the perpetrators displayed prior to the occurrence of their assault that in retrospect appeared to have been warning signs of impending problems in their relationship. These attitudes and behaviors of the perpetrator, appearing singularly and in interaction with each other, include the following:

- Anger
- Aggressiveness
- A preoccupation with sex
- Control or possessiveness
- Disrespect for women in general and for the victim in particular

Comments from acquaintance rape survivors will be used to illustrate each of these themes.

Anger. A survivor recalls the anger she experienced from her boyfriend who later raped her:

His anger seemed to be always just below the surface.

Another survivor writes:

I grew to become fearful of his anger, or more properly I should say his rage. I recall he could fly off in a rage at what seemed insignificant things.

A respondent from Texas describes her acquaintance's attempts to control her, a theme to be discussed later, and his angry reaction when she failed to comply with his control:

At first he appeared very nice. As time progressed, he used flattery to get my attention. He would give me things or try to buy things for me. When I didn't accept them, he became angry.

Numerous respondents commented that they complied with their friend's demands simply out of fear of his anger. A survivor who was raped by a boyfriend described how he would pout and become angry if he did not get his way, including his desire to have sex. Although initially she complied with his wishes, as she began to resist his advances and demands for sex without regard to her feelings, he became angry and raped her.

Aggressiveness. Numerous survivors remarked about their perpetrator's aggressiveness. Underlying this attitude appeared to be the feeling that what the perpetrator wanted was most important. His attitude showed a distinct lack of respect for the feelings of his female acquaintance. A respondent from Georgia describes her perpetrator, as she now thinks back on her assault by this acquaintance.

> There was a forcefulness about him on many issues—not just relative to sex.

Another survivor writes:

> He was a fast mover and rough—not sensitive and caring but more of an attitude of "I'm going to get *my* needs met."

Two additional survivors describe their acquaintances who later assaulted them:

> He would constantly say how strong and powerful or dangerous and tough he was.

> He acted very pushy and was very negative around me. He kept putting me down and making me feel very insecure. My saying, "No," and pushing him away almost seemed to encourage him.

A Preoccupation With Sex. In many instances the perpetrator's aggressiveness was associated with his expectation and demand for sex. Survivors described their acquaintances, who later became their assailants, as preoccupied with sex. In some instances, the survivor had consented to sex with the perpetrator on earlier occasions and there was the expectancy that sexual activity would continue whenever the perpetrator wished. Of the 236 survivors, 25% (60) reported previous sexual activity with the perpetrator consisting of kissing, fondling, and, in some instances, sexual intercourse.

A young woman who was dating a physician during his internship describes her earlier sexual activity with him and her eventual rape:

> There was sexual activity prior to the rape between my boyfriend and me involving kissing and touching but no intercourse. The effects were confusing. He didn't like being told to stop or "No." Sometimes I felt I had an octopus on my hands because he didn't like being pushed away. "I'm a man; I'm a lion," were the phrases he used to describe himself.
>
> My uncle was with the FBI and I had been involved in talks and demonstrations on protecting oneself. However, the night the rape occurred, I turned numb. I couldn't move, as though everything was taken away from me. I tried several times to push him away with my feet only to be pulled to the foot of the bed and hurt more. He held my arms down and I couldn't move them. He was holding tightly onto them.

Another respondent writes:

> He would focus on sexuality, sexual things, such as my body rather than my personality.

Another survivor recalls:

> He brought up sex or sexual behavior a lot in our conversations.

Some men incorrectly feel they must be aggressive in their relationship with women. They hold this role expectation for themselves and falsely perceive that their female acquaintances hold the same expectation of them. A study of sexually aggressive dating attitudes supports this inaccurate role perception (Dull & Giacopassi, 1987). Researchers report that dating attitudes of 500 undergraduate students differed significantly by gender. Males were far more likely than females to hold attitudes that condone aggressive sexual behavior. Two thirds of all male respondents in the research sample indicated ambivalence toward or acceptance of the statement, "For some females, physical aggressiveness by the male is a necessary prelude to the acceptance of love and affection."

Research also documents that some men feel a woman's role in the dating relationship is one of setting limits on their sexually aggressive behavior. In a study of male and female college students, researchers found males tended to believe that if rape occurred on a date, it was due at least in part to the female's failure to exercise adequate control (Bridges & McGrail, 1989; Muehlenhard & Linton, 1987). Studies also show that men tend to perceive more sexual intent in social situations than females and that the male's misunderstanding of the female's behavior or desires is a contributing factor to date rape (Abbey, 1982; Abbey & Melby, 1983). These findings do not remove the responsibility that men must assume for their behavior. However, the findings also emphasize the importance of women giving clear and unambiguous messages regarding their intent in dating relationships. Unfortunately, even when women give a very clear message regarding the limitations they wish respected relative to sexual activity on a date, some men still do not accept the message.

Control or Possessiveness. Repeatedly the theme of the perpetrator's need to control his female acquaintance was expressed in survivors' comments. Following are examples:

> He had an obsession about having me all to himself, wanting to control me totally. He would become very upset if he couldn't control my actions.

Another survivor describes the controlling behavior of her friend. She engages in self-blame as she recalls the behavior:

> He behaved very possessively toward me. By this I mean he wouldn't let others around me when we were out—to talk to me, dance with me, and so forth. One time he pinned me against the bar with his

arms around me when he turned to talk to someone else, as if he did not want me to get away. When I would go to the bathroom, he would ask, "Are you coming right back?" At the time, it didn't seem like that big of a deal. In retrospect, it seems like a well-laid plan. I feel so foolish for not seeing this behavior as being indicative of extreme controlling behavior. I'm a counselor. I should have been able to pick up on this.

In the preface to this book the statement was made to the effect that violence occurring in the courtship/acquaintance relationship may be a precursor to the high rates of violence seen in the marital relationship. The theme of men feeling they must control their female acquaintances, as evidenced in the preceding survivors' comments, is a common theme found by mental health professionals working with men who batter their wives (Walker, 1984). For example, a husband may call home at various times during the day and find that his wife does not answer the phone. He continues to call at frequent intervals. He may even leave his job to go home to check on his wife. Although she may be visiting a neighbor or running an errand, the husband's need to control his wife leads him to think that she may be with another man. Later, he may confront his wife about her absence and falsely accuse her of infidelity. These confrontations are often marked by physical battering.

An acquaintance rape survivor reported that she initially found her date's "protective" behavior to be flattering; however, after the assault she took a different view of the behavior and now regards it as a form of entrapment.

The emphasis on protection some perpetrators displayed toward their dates, who later became the victims of their assaults, was conceptualized by other survivors as jealousy. The following survivors describe their experiences:

He was very jealous. He didn't like me to be talking to or eating lunch with other men. He would always phrase it in terms of, "You deserve better."

He would not let me go anywhere without him. He would listen to my telephone calls.

He had a lot of very definite ideas about how I should behave, such as if I were too outspoken at a gathering or if I ever used slang or swore. As I look back on this now, this behavior seemed like a subtle means of control and an attempt to undermine my self-confidence.

A Lack of Respect for the Victim. As survivors looked back on their assault, they recalled their discomfort with their assailant's lack of respect for women in general that in turn was a reflection of his attitude toward them as an individual.

He talked about women as nothing but sex objects. He would say women were all the same mentally—dumb, but different when it came to sex.

He would make jokes that consisted of sexual remarks regarding women. He would talk about single women and refer to their sexual behavior and "what they needed." His conversation frequently included sexual references to my body.

He showed disrespect toward women. He thought Dice Clay and his vulgar jokes about women were extremely funny. He would speak badly about his former girlfriend—called her names like "cunt," "slut."

He frequently made me feel very naive and inferior, but at the time I admired and looked up to him because he was older than me and he seemed so smart. Now as I look back on this, it was his attempt to control me.

Summary

In this chapter survivors have described a variety of settings where their sexual assault by an acquaintance occurred. In many instances their assault took place in the victim's or perpetrator's home. As survivors looked back on their sexual assault by an acquaintance, they identified the following perpetrator attitudes and behaviors that in retrospect may have been warning signs of impending problems: anger, aggressiveness, a preoccupation with sex, control or possessiveness, and a lack of respect for women in general and for the victim in particular. These attitudes and behaviors may be regarded as warning signs for women in preventing sexual assault by an acquaintance.

*The rape I experienced from my boyfriend
is like a huge dark cloud always hanging
above my head.*
—An acquaintance rape survivor

4 Survivors' Response to Their Assault

The perpetrators of the rape, as has been emphasized previously, were not strangers but acquaintances. A friend or an acquaintance is someone you can trust. To be sexually assaulted by someone you trust represents a betrayal, as the title of this book portrays. The theme of this chapter is the survivors' response to their assault. Specifically, the chapter will focus on the following questions: Did survivors identify their sexual assault by an acquaintance as rape? Was the rape reported to authorities? Were survivors able to discuss their sexual assault with anyone? Did they prosecute their perpetrators? Acquaintance rape survivors will answer these questions in their own words so that you can understand how and why victims respond as they do to sexual assault from an acquaintance.

Identifying What Occurred

The way survivors identify an assault they experience may influence the action they take following the attack. Whether or not the victims even were aware of the phenomenon of acquaintance rape may influence their response to what occurred. For many individuals, the word *rape* only implies sexual assault by a stranger. They are not aware that sexual assault by an acquaintance is also labeled as rape. Of the 236 participants in this research, 58% (135) indicated they had never heard of the term *acquaintance rape* before it happened to them. Thus, only 42% were even aware of the term. One must remember in interpreting these data that for 27% (62) of the survivors the rape occurred 2 or more years ago. Because the term acquaintance rape has only been used in recent years, many of the survivors may not have been familiar with it.

Participants also were asked whether or not they defined their own experience of being forced to engage in sexual activity without their consent with an acquaintance as acquaintance rape at the time it happened. Of the 236 respondents, 61% (143) did not define their own experience as rape. A theme running throughout survivors' comments regarding their rape was that they did not realize the assault they had experienced was rape until sometime later when they participated in a class, read something about acquaintance rape in the newspaper, or saw a TV program that educated them on the subject.

The failure of respondents in this research to identify their sexual assault as rape is not unusual and is supported by other research data. Researchers found in a study of 206 female college students that the vast majority of these women failed to label themselves as acquaintance rape victims, even though 58% of the sample had experienced sexual intercourse against their wishes (Amick & Calhoun, 1987). Similarly, researchers report on the basis of a study of college women raped by a stranger and a comparative group raped by an acquaintance that whereas 55% of these women assaulted by a stranger considered their experience rape, only 23% of those raped by an acquaintance did so (Koss et al., 1988).

The failure of acquaintance rape victims to recognize or acknowledge that they have been sexually assaulted emphasizes the important role education plays in the prevention of acquaintance rape. Education about acquaintance rape will enable survivors to identify sexual activity in which they are forced to engage against their wishes as rape and to report such activity to authorities.

Initial Response to the Assault

What was the initial response of victims to their sexual assault by an acquaintance? Survivors describe how they initially reacted.

Reporting the Assault to Police

On the basis of the previous data indicating that the majority of the victims did not define their sexual assault by an acquaintance as rape, it is not surprising that nearly two thirds of them did not report their assault to authorities. Of the 236 survivors, 72% (170 individuals) did not report the assault to authorities compared to 28% (66 individuals) who did.

Researchers have found in comparing victims of stranger rape with victims of acquaintance rape relative to whether or not they reported their assault to police, that less than 2% of the acquaintance rape victims reported their assault compared to 21% of those raped by a stranger (Koss et al., 1988).

Why don't acquaintance rape victims report their assault to authorities? Fear, guilt, and shame to a large extent account for their failure to report. These factors also are associated with the self-blame in which the victims engage. Self-blame is a recurring theme in survivors' comments who did and who did not report their assault. In some instances, the self-blame was even reinforced by family or friends who, on hearing of the assault, overtly or covertly blamed the victim for what occurred. "Why did you invite him to your apartment?" "Why did you go to his house?" "Why didn't you run away from him?" "Were you drinking at the time?" "Had you had sex before with him?" These and similar questions, although on the surface appear to be asking for information, in essence are blaming the victim for what happened.

Although some survivors reported their assault, they did so fearfully, realizing society's tendency to blame the victim when rape occurs. Some survivors did not report their assault to the police for fear their name would appear in the newspaper and they would be victimized by those who saw this. In a few instances, the perpetrator even threatened the victim if she were to report the assault.

A survivor of rape from a fellow employee and friend states her reason for not reporting her assault. Notice how the survivor engages in self-blame:

> I didn't report the rape because I felt guilty, thinking I brought it on. He also was a friend and I was having trouble believing he had raped me. I also was scared to go to court because I figured I would go through hell in the courtroom and he would get away with it anyway.

A survivor sexually molested as an adolescent by a teenage boyfriend writes:

> I still have trouble thinking of what happened to me as rape. I still have a hard time calling it rape aloud. I've always thought of rape as intercourse with a lot of violence but my experience was fondling. Rape victims don't get up and go to school the next day as I did.

Another survivor who was forced to engage in sexual activities with a male friend without her consent comments:

> No, I never reported the rape or told anyone. Who would have cared? That's how I felt about it.

A college student raped by another student and coworker on a part-time job writes:

> I didn't report the rape to authorities because I believed it was my fault for voluntarily going with him.

Although some victims did report their assault to the police, the way the report was handled further victimized them. A 29-year-old woman was forced to submit to sexual intercourse and to fellate her perpetrator, a male friend whom she had met through mutual friends. Following the assault, she immediately told her boyfriend. She writes:

> My boyfriend reported my rape to the police department before we went to the hospital. The dispatcher actually hung up in my boyfriend's face because he was loud and upset. Two officers

came—a female who was supportive, and a male who said, "Usually
if women are out at this time of night, it was their fault." This made
me feel worse.

A young woman writes about her experience of reporting her
rape to the police:

> I reported the rape to the police 3 days after it happened. I was in
> shock prior to this and had no idea what I was going to do about it.
> I decided to report it because my rights as a person had been violated
> and I had to try to do something about it. Sexual Assault Services
> helped me contact the police and I went in and gave a statement to
> a detective. No investigation was made; they never arrested the man;
> they destroyed evidence. All of these things hurt my case. My expe-
> rience with the police was that no one wanted to help me. They
> wanted to make decisions for me and patronize me. They were
> insensitive and very unprofessional.

The anticipated response from authorities was a critical factor
that kept some victims from reporting their assault and their actual
response prevented others from continuing to pursue their assailant's prosecution. A survivor who decided to prosecute her assailant
described the process as one where she felt as if she, rather than her
assailant, was on trial. Another survivor vividly described the court-
room process. She writes:

> My experience in the courtroom was like being raped all over again,
> only this time it was worse because I was in front of a room full of
> people. It was very traumatic being on the witness stand and telling
> everyone what happened and being treated very badly by the perpe-
> trator's lawyer.

A survivor, beaten and raped by an acquaintance, reported her
assault to the police. The police came to her home in response to her
report. She described the humiliating experience of the police taking
pictures of marks on her nude body.

A 17-year-old woman was gang raped by three acquaintances of
her boyfriend. She had met these men in a bar that she and her boyfriend frequented. On leaving the bar and with her boyfriend not being

able to find his car keys, these friends volunteered to drive her home so she could meet her curfew. Rather than driving her home, they took her to an isolated area and raped her. She writes that she did not want to report the rape. Rather, she only wanted to stay in bed. Her mother insisted the rape be reported:

> My mother insisted my father take me to the police. He did. The police said, "It's your word against the three of them: You will ruin their lives and, after all, they are veterans." I shall never forget the look in my father's eyes when he gathered up my bloody clothes and we left.

Seeking Medical Assistance

The same number of individuals who did not report the rape to authorities (72% or 170 individuals) did not seek medical assistance following the acquaintance rape.

A respondent who sought medical assistance describes her frightening experience:

> I sought medical assistance but it was one of the most difficult aspects of the whole assault. I just wanted to crawl into a dark, quiet place and be left alone. Instead I was under bright lights—exposed, poked, swabbed, looked at. My pubic hair was combed and they kept my clothes for evidence. I did not have control again! It felt like I was again violated. The doctor was kind and soft spoken and treated me with respect. But, I just wanted to be left alone. It felt like I had walked into yet another nightmare.

Rape crisis counselors were helpful to other survivors when they sought medical assistance:

> I had to wait 3 hours for an examination at the hospital. A rape crisis volunteer who was very nice helped me keep my mind off what happened. The doctor and nurse also were nice to me.

> I sought medical assistance the day following my rape. I think the experience was as positive as it could have been under the circumstances. The hospital called a rape task force volunteer. She stayed with me the whole time. I understand that I was fortunate. Most

people experience the hospital as the second rape. I did feel somewhat violated at the hospital because they had to do an evidence
kit in case I decided to prosecute in the future.

I sought medical assistance following the rape. I had an examination
at a local hospital with the assistance of a rape crisis volunteer—a
very supportive person.

Rape survivors frequently feel they are victimized by the medical
personnel they contact following their assault. Research using samples of medical students responding to narratives of three types of
patients—a stereotypical rape victim, a victim of a robbery, and a
victim of a rape by someone known to the victim—found that female
medical students had more favorable attitudes toward the victims
than did male medical students. Also, male medical students demonstrated more victim-blaming attitudes in the narrative where the
victim knew her assailant when compared with their responses to
the narratives involving a stereotypical rape victim or a robbery
victim. The findings suggest that medical students, most of whom
are males, have personal belief systems regarding what constitutes
a "real" rape that may in turn have an impact on their future role as
physicians when treating such victims (Best, Dansky, & Kilpatrick,
1992). In light of these findings, acquaintance rape victims may have
difficulty being perceived as real rape victims for the assault they
experienced and may sense blame from an attending physician and
allied medical personnel.

Other survivors reported positive experiences when they sought
medical assistance following their assault. Some survivors attributed their positive experience at the hospital to the fact that the
attending physician was a woman rather than a man. This was very
important to them in light of the assault they had just experienced
from a male. Also, they felt that a woman could better understand
how they were feeling at the time.

Prosecuting the Perpetrator

Respondents were asked if they prosecuted the perpetrator. Only
45 of the 236 victims attempted to prosecute their perpetrator. The

greatest number of survivors, 80% (189), did not prosecute their assailant.

Why did so few of the survivors report their rape to authorities or even attempt to prosecute their perpetrators? The comments of survivors participating in the research help us understand their reluctance to report the assault or to prosecute their assailant.

A college coed, raped by an athlete at the school she attended, wrote that she didn't report the rape to authorities because she blamed herself for breaking all the rules "nice girls" should follow in meeting and dating men. She states she couldn't admit to anyone that she had been so stupid as to put herself in the situation she had been in. Rather than report the rape and prosecute her assailant, this survivor blamed herself for what happened.

Another survivor answered with one word the question as to whether or not she prosecuted her perpetrator. Her brief cynical response perhaps reflects self-blame for what occurred in addition to the response she anticipated from the authorities, who also would probably blame her. She writes: "Ha!"

A 26-year-old woman was forced to have sexual relations with a male friend she met through an outpatient alcoholism treatment program. They were friends for nearly a year before he raped her. She writes:

> I did my best to get the man into court. The county attorney turned down the case, so I pursued civil action. This did not work out because I had no money for legal fees, and Legal Aid does not handle rape cases.
>
> I tried for several months to get the case reopened in criminal court, writing letters and meeting with the county attorney, victim/witness coordinator, director of public safety, and the chief of detectives. After 11 months, a new assistant county attorney became interested and decided she would take my case. We went to trial 17 months after the rape.
>
> My perpetrator's lawyer, a public defender, lied, misquoted the laws, and ripped me to shreds on the stand.
>
> Ultimately, the inadequate laws and the poorly worded statutes for sexual misconduct gave the jury no choice but to find the man not guilty on all four charges—two charges for penetration and two for contact.

> After the trial, the perpetrator and his lawyer went over to the jury box to shake the jurors' hands. None of them would even look at the man or his lawyer. They all just turned and walked out of the courtroom. They *knew* I was telling the truth and yet they let him off.
> It was devastating and yet not surprising because I had been seeing the helping professionals and the system of justice for 17 months and knew what my chances were going into the trial. My feeling was that I had to fight for my rights and for the principle involved.

The literature on victims' decisions to prosecute in rape cases generally focuses on their willingness to follow through in prosecuting the assailant (Black, 1970; Williams, 1981). Research, however, also emphasizes the important role detectives play in processing rape victims' attempts to prosecute their assailant. Using participant observations and interviews with detectives as well as analyzing documents and reports in 364 stranger and 223 acquaintance rape cases, researchers found that detectives inevitably influence survivors' decisions to prosecute. Three factors are identified in the research that directly or indirectly affect police officers' and their influence on rape victims in their attempt to prosecute their assailants: (a) Women who have violated traditional or stereotypical female sex-role norms are often discouraged by the police to prosecute their assailant; (b) The race of the victim and offender, their occupational status, and how well the offender represents the conventional or stereotypical views of an offender has an affect on the extent to which officers encourage victims in their pursuit of prosecution; and (c) Police screening decisions of cases where prosecution is encouraged or discouraged are influenced by the need to allocate scarce resources (Kerstetter & Van Winkle, 1990). Thus, circumstances surrounding the case affect the way in which detectives may encourage or discourage survivors in their attempts to prosecute their assailant. These factors highlight the importance of rape crisis centers providing anticipatory guidance and support to victims as they contemplate prosecution of their perpetrators lest they be discouraged to prosecute after they make an initial contact with the police department.

A victim's hesitancy or uncertainty regarding her intent to prosecute of itself can be a factor that influences the way police respond to rape complaints. If the victim does not want to prosecute, obviously it is difficult for the police to investigate the case. Even if the victim were forced to participate in the investigation, she may set up barriers for the police in their investigation by withholding information or presenting ambiguous information. Police generally have far more cases than they can handle and thus are reluctant to pursue the investigation of rape cases where the victim is uncooperative. Also, police experience suggests that a face-saving way of recanting a complaint is to decide not to pursue it. Thus, unless there is independent evidence apart from what the victim states, a case will not be investigated.

Sometimes detectives use the victim's lack of enthusiasm or interest in pursuing a case for their own advantage. Detectives do not like to be associated with unsolved cases. Thus, a detective may overtly or covertly discourage a victim from pursuing prosecution, especially if the victim does not seem firm in her resolve to prosecute. The detective may do this by describing to the victim her personal costs in pursuing conviction, including the amount of time this will take, the risks of exposing herself to family and friends in the process of presenting testimony in court, and possible long-term effects on her personal character. On the other hand, if the detective wants to pursue prosecution based on available evidence, the detective may appeal to the victim's conscience to pursue the investigation to prevent an assault on another woman (Kerstetter, 1990).

Some survivors, however, did report their sexual assault by an acquaintance and successfully prosecuted their assailant. A 35-year-old woman raped by a male acquaintance writes:

> I prosecuted my rapist. My trial took 2 days and I was a nervous wreck. They found him guilty, and he received 15 years. I hope they keep him in prison for the whole 15 years because he deserves to spend the entire time in prison for what he did to me.

A 32-year-old businesswoman, the mother of several small children, who was sexually molested by a family friend and employee, also experienced positive results when she prosecuted her assailant. She reports:

Yes, I prosecuted him. Initially he was arrested and charged with
aggravated sexual battery, lewd and lascivious behavior. He entered
a plea bargain at the preliminary hearing. Rather than wait 8 months
for a jury trial, I wanted to get it all over with. Therefore, I accepted
his plea to lewd and lascivious behavior. He was put on 2 years
supervised probation and ordered to not contact my family or myself directly or indirectly. He was also ordered to seek counseling
following a psychological evaluation.

Telling Others

Survivors were asked if they had told anyone about their rape.
They were requested to share the reactions of those whom they told
about the trauma they had experienced. Of the 236 respondents, 97%
(226) had told someone about their sexual assault.

The reaction of those who heard what happened was largely
positive and supportive. Undoubtedly, this positive response relates
to the survivors being selective of whom they told. One survivor
clearly states this:

> I am very careful who knows anything about my personal life and
> what I did or did not do. I can say that I was raped but I also know
> who I choose to speak to about this. Details are my own business!
> General remarks are OK, but it depends on the audience.

Another survivor writes about her experience in sharing the
information on her rape. In essence, the survivor appears to be
saying that people may be accepting on the surface when they hear
that you have been raped by an acquaintance, but underneath they
may be blaming you for what happened and allowing this blame to
spread to other areas of your life:

> I'm careful now with whom I share the information of my rape
> because they can use that to discount anything you say.

Survivors were asked to identify their relationship to the person
or persons whom they told about the rape. When survivors told a
close male friend about the rape by an acquaintance, several types

of responses were noted in the data. Some males responded with extreme anger against the perpetrator. For example, a survivor who had experienced sexual assault from an acquaintance shared this information many years later with her boyfriend. He became very angry and wanted to take revenge; however, because of the passage of time this was not possible. This survivor understood how powerless her boyfriend felt on learning of her sexual assault. She interpreted his reaction as supportive and caring.

An opposite response, one lacking in empathy and understanding, was experienced by some survivors when they told male friends about their acquaintance rape. This response may have been due to several factors. Some males holding stereotypical views of male/ female relationships may have identified with the aggressor in that they felt the assailant had a right to expect sexual gratification. Others may have blamed the survivor for what happened as a defense for not taking responsibility for their own behavior, had they been in such a situation.

Finally, some males on hearing about a survivor's rape by an acquaintance were unable to respond. Survivors found this response to be confusing. A survivor, raped 2 years earlier by a college classmate, writes:

> I told my current boyfriend about the rape. He has been very supportive of it. However, I think he has also been at a loss for words and is not really sure how to react.

When survivors told their parents about their rape by an acquaintance, they reported their parents responded by being "upset" and "distraught." Following this, the subject of their rape became a closed issue between them in that it was no longer discussed. This reaction left the survivor alone with her feelings and the impact of the trauma on her life. The imposed silence was interpreted by some survivors that perhaps their parents were in part blaming them for what occurred. However, because the parents chose to deal with the assault as a "closed issue," this could not be discussed further with them.

Female friends with whom the survivor shared her traumatic experiences were described as being very supportive and understanding.

Female friends, undoubtedly similar in age to the survivor, appeared to be able to empathize or place themselves in the survivor's position. An interesting side effect of a survivor telling female friends about her rape is illustrated in a survivor's comment. After she told them about what happened to her, she realized she was not alone in the assault she had experienced:

> I told my three girlfriends and they *all* confessed that they too had been raped by an acquaintance.

A survivor from Georgia, raped by a friend of her boyfriend, provides a commentary on the previous comment:

> I wonder how many women are raped every day by acquaintances but the information is never known. We keep it a secret. As society says, "It's never his fault, even if it is."

Researchers, using groups of college women raped by strangers and acquaintances, reported the following reactions to the rape (Koss et al., 1988). In response to the question as to whether they told anyone about their rape, the researchers found that 65% of the women raped by nonromantic acquaintances discussed their experience with someone compared to 59.4% of the women raped by casual dates, 44.5% by steady dates, and 43.8% by husbands or other family members. The data suggest that the closer the relationship of the assailant to the victim, the less likely she was to discuss her sexual assault with anyone. This may be due to factors such as embarrassment and self-blame—the latter occurring in the context of feeling she should have known better or should not have trusted the acquaintance. The same researchers found that women raped by a stranger were more likely to discuss their experience with someone, to have sought services from a rape crisis center, and to have reported their assault to the police.

A response survivors in our research frequently received from others with whom they shared the fact they had been sexually assaulted by an acquaintance was that they should "get on with their life." This advice was interpreted by survivors as a message regarding how they should handle their victimization—namely, to forget about it, pretend it never happened, to not dwell on it. This response reflects the discomfort of the person hearing about the sexual assault. The rape account from an acquaintance was so dissonant that the hearer did not want to think about it. This response from the hearer also encourages the survivor to engage in denial about the event and its potential impact on her life. Unfortunately, a trauma of this nature, the violation of the basic trust a survivor has in an acquaintance, is not handled by forgetting it or, in psychological terms, by suppressing the event. Rather, the human psyche continues to deal with the trauma, recalling it as similar situations arise that provoke it to consciousness and reprocessing the event, often associating its impact with other problems-in-living the survivor may be experiencing. This highlights the importance of the recovery process for survivors, a focus of a later chapter.

For some survivors, working with other victims of interpersonal violence has helped them work through their own problems resulting from their acquaintance rape. A survivor comments:

> Even though I didn't go through specific therapy following my rape, I did volunteer work with battered women and other abuse victims/ survivors. This helped me a great deal with the issue of trust, especially with men, with which I was struggling.

A survivor talks about her recovery and the need to move on from the initial trauma. However, this does not imply pretending the event never happened:

> I have told others about my rape. Most are shocked that I have a good life, family, and am not forever branded. I teach many others who have experienced similar trauma that you have control as to whether you remain a victim or go past your wound and be happy. There is a lot of trauma around. We can concentrate and hold on to it or move forward, leaving the garbage behind us.

Summary

This chapter has reported the immediate response of survivors to their sexual assault by an acquaintance. Many survivors were not familiar with the label of acquaintance rape and thus, as would be expected, did not identify their own assault as a rape. Of those who did report their rape to authorities, who did seek medical assistance, or who even prosecuted the perpetrator, some found that police and legal personnel demonstrated little empathy and compassion for them. Survivors often felt they were covertly being blamed for what happened from the way in which authorities phrased their questions about the rape. Survivors also found that family members and friends were uncomfortable with what had happened to them. This discomfort at times was expressed in the admonition to simply forget what happened. However, forgetting is not possible for the acquaintance rape survivor as she continues to wrestle with the impact of this trauma on her life, the focus of the next chapter.

It's very confusing. He was my date. He was supposed to respect me. Instead he sodomized me.
—An acquaintance rape survivor

5 The Assault's Impact on the Survivor

One may easily be able to identify with victims of stranger rape regarding the impact this trauma has on their lives in terms of their fear of going places alone and their distrust of strangers. However, some may not regard the impact of acquaintance rape as seriously because the victim knows her assailant. Thus, the assumption may be falsely made that the effects of acquaintance rape may not be as serious as those of stranger rape. Research shows, however, that when women raped by a stranger are compared to those raped by an acquaintance in terms of the rape's impact on their lives, there was no difference in the two groups. Both groups scored similarly on measures of depression, anxiety, quality of subsequent relationships, and sexual satisfaction following their rape (Koss et al., 1988).

This chapter will focus on survivors' descriptions of how their sexual assault by an acquaintance affected their lives. Survivors' responses were categorized into three areas: their ability to trust others, their ability to be intimate with others, and their ability to deal with the anger experienced from the rape.

Trusting Others

If someone whom you trust commits a violent act against you, will you be able to trust others again in the future? Feelings of distrust may transfer from this trauma to similar situations. Individuals who have experienced what they perceive as a traumatic event, for example, being attacked by a dog while walking down a sidewalk or being mugged by a stranger, report for years following this event they experience anxiety when they are in a similar situation. This reaction may be understood as an erosion of a basic sense of trust. A survivor describes her dilemma:

> The man who raped me was someone I knew and trusted. How could I possibly trust anyone again?

Women who are survivors of acquaintance rape may most severely feel the impact of their victimization in terms of the erosion of trust, specifically in subsequent relationships with men. This loss of trust is demonstrated in the following survivors' comments:

> I was not married at the time of the rape and for years I did not develop positive relationships with men. There was no trust.

> I am very distrustful of others, particularly men. When a guy comes up to me to talk and to be friendly, my "radar" is working full force. Even if he seems nice, I try not to be left alone with him. I have pretty well gotten over the panic if a man sits next to me, even in church.

> I no longer date and have no expectations for marriage now or in the future. I keep my thoughts and feelings to myself. I limit the amount of information anyone has about me to factual accounts of education and work experience.

The violation of a basic sense of trust in others that occurred as a result of the acquaintance rape affects even the survivor's interpersonal relationship with their spouse. The inability to trust others for some survivors was a significant factor in the eventual break-up of their marriage. A survivor describes how the acquaintance rape affects her marriage:

My husband is very understanding and supportive, but I know it's hard on him to see me this way. He knows to be very careful, not to startle me, or come up and grab me from behind. We've done a lot of modifying in our lives.

A young woman raped as a college student by a fellow student writes the following:

I was a virgin when I was raped and unfortunately had not experienced trust or intimacy prior to the assault. I did begin an intimate relationship a few months later but did not disclose the rape until almost a year into the relationship. I stayed in the relationship for over a year but in all that time I constantly built a wall between us to keep myself from feeling vulnerable. I remember constantly testing my boyfriend; for example, will he still love me if he knows about this, or that, or something else? I was so fearful of allowing myself to completely trust someone that I eventually pushed him away. I've just recently come to associate my behavior with my feelings about myself stemming from the rape.

Intimacy

Not only the ability to trust but especially to be intimate with a person of the opposite sex is severely affected when an individual is sexually assaulted by an acquaintance. A survivor describes how her rape has affected her current relationship with a male friend:

I cannot have sex without remembering the rape. I feel like someone is making an object out of me and that I play no active role in the intercourse. I have been in the same relationship for the past year and really trust my partner now. But before this relationship, I was extremely afraid of being in a romantic one-on-one situation with a man. Intimacy can be a big problem. There was one time when the two of us were alone and he commented on how nice it was to be all alone with me. I panicked! I looked at him and he didn't look the same anymore. I was very afraid to be there alone with him at that moment even though I knew him so well.

Survivors report difficulty in their sexual relationships with their spouses, stemming from their sexual assault by an acquaintance:

> Sex with my husband is very, very hard. I can be looking right into his eyes, but the moment he touches me sexually, he isn't my husband anymore. He's the man who raped me.

Another survivor was 15 years old at the time she was assaulted by her 17-year-old boyfriend. She had been abused by him on several occasions but would continue to date him because he would cry and say he was sorry for what he had done. Eventually, he raped her. She describes the impact her victimization had on her sexuality and, in turn, on her marriage. She also comments on the help she and her husband received from therapy:

> Through the abusive relationship, I was taught that I existed only for sex. I felt as though if I couldn't be good for anything else, I would be very good at sex. My present husband was the first person that I went out with following the abusive relationship. My boundaries were gone. I became promiscuous with my (then future) husband early in our dating relationship. I never told him "No." I don't think I would have said "No" to anyone at that point. Thank God my future husband valued me more than I valued myself.
>
> Throughout our dating and early marital relationship, I used sex to try to fix any problems between us. Anytime my husband touched me or winked, and so on, I responded sexually. It was overkill. He gradually stopped touching me because he did not want sex that often. I then felt rejected and was even more sexually aggressive. It was a vicious circle. I began being unfaithful to my husband—looking for validation of my attractiveness, and so on. My self-esteem sank even lower. My husband grew even more distant and I felt even worse. It has taken *much work* on both of our parts, but the intimacy between us now is wonderful. We had to go back to square one and learn to communicate our needs, wishes, and so on to each other—something that should have occurred before our sexual relationship began. For so long, I had functioned as a "sex machine." I worked really hard to be good at sex and to fulfill my partner. I worked so hard at it that I was unable to relax and reach orgasm, which in turn frustrated my husband. Our marriage has made great strides through the help of therapy.

A respondent, raped by an acquaintance, has had three unsuccessful marriages. She writes:

> I am currently unmarried and recently broke up with my boyfriend. I am terrified to get into another relationship because they all end the same way and I am left feeling dirty and coldhearted. I find I cannot truly love. I don't seem to know how. The intimacy is fine for a while. Then, something happens inside of me and not long after, I don't want him to touch me anymore. There are horrible memories inside me wanting to get out but there is no escape. I sometimes don't think I can go on. This is like a huge dark cloud always hanging above my head.

Many survivors also appreciatively spoke of supportive, patient, and understanding mates who have been helpful to them in coping with the impact of their acquaintance rape, especially in the area of sexual intimacy. A young woman in her 20s, raped by her husband's best friend, writes:

> The rape has drawn my husband and I very close together. He is my biggest supporter. He is still full of rage knowing his best friend did this to me, but he is getting through it with me. His trust for me is so strong. We have hang-ups on sex that aren't his fault. It's what happens to me—like sometimes I freeze up. I feel nothing and I don't want to be touched. It is something that I am going to need a lot of therapy with. My husband understands and is very patient with me.

Studies show that sexual abuse survivors often react along a continuum of responses in terms of their sexual functioning. The extreme points on the continuum are—at one end not wanting anything to do with sex to, at the opposite end of the continuum, being sexually compulsive (Ellis, Atkeson, & Calhoun, 1981; Frank, Turner, & Stewart, 1980; Kilpatrick, Veronen, & Best, 1985; Ruch & Chandler, 1983).

A survivor describes her avoidance of sex based on her rape by a fellow employee:

> I don't know if I can ever experience intimacy or sex again. It turns my stomach just thinking of a man touching me.

The opposite end of the continuum—namely, compulsive sexuality or sexual acting out—is another response to the rape. This behavior may be understood from several perspectives. The behavior may represent the survivor's unconscious efforts to master, overcome, or deny her feelings of powerlessness, shame, and rage that resulted from her sexual victimization. The elements of distrust, danger, and physical or emotional abuse that were present in the assault may be recreated in the survivor's repeated sexual encounters. The sexual compulsivity may also represent the survivor's confusion with the boundaries that delineate affection, sex, and abuse.

The promiscuity or sexual acting out the survivor engages in may also relate to the low self-esteem she feels following the sexual assault. Feelings of worthlessness may influence her choices of acquaintances and associates, which can in turn make her vulnerable to further sexual victimization. A respondent raped by an acquaintance as an adolescent, when asked how she felt the rape affected her dating patterns, responded:

> I began to only date guys that I had no chance of a future with so I wouldn't get close and get hurt. And I could only have sex with them if I had been drinking first.

A young woman in her late teens, raped by a high school classmate, describes her sexual response to the rape:

> From the time I was raped until just very recently, I was turning into a real tramp. I went out with several older men and I always ended up in their bed. There was no intimacy; it always was strictly sex. We never meant anything to each other. Even though I didn't have any real trust in any of these men, I was still willing to have sex with them because I would numb out.

This survivor goes on to contrast her relationship to men now after becoming involved in counseling for her dysfunctional sexual behavior:

I am not married but fortunately I have found a very wonderful man who was the one responsible for getting me to seek counseling. I trust him wholeheartedly. We are not yet intimate. We are now getting to know each other properly and slowly. We both feel we have a great future together.

Another position on the continuum of responses to sexual intimacy was reported by survivors. Survivors described themselves as "disassociating" during sex following their rape by an acquaintance —namely, they acted as if they were not participating in the sexual act with their mate or that their mate was actually having sex with someone else.

Anger

Participants in the research made reference repeatedly to the anger they felt toward the perpetrator. The anger for some was expressed at men in general. A survivor writes:

I do not trust men. They are all sex maniacs in one way or another. After the rape, I set out to become just like them. I used alcohol to numb myself and then went out to "get them"—to screw them without any love or consciousness—to use them the way they used me.

Because the sample for the research was collected from rape crisis centers, it may be assumed that the respondents had been or were currently involved in some type of helping relationship, such as individual or group therapy, or were participating in a support group for rape survivors. This may account for their awareness of the anger they felt.

Some acquaintance rape survivors deny their anger and blame themselves for this victimization. This self-blame, which we have found in earlier comments of survivors, is seen in such statements as, "I should never have accepted the invitation to go to his apartment," or "I should have attempted harder to resist." Family members and friends may reinforce the survivor's denial of anger and add to the self-blame by overtly blaming her for what occurred, or by remaining silent about the rape, which may be interpreted by the survivors that they are being blamed for what happened (Blake-White & Kline, 1985).

Dr. Harriet Goldhor Lerner (1985), in her book *The Dance of Anger*, describes the way many women who have been victims of various types of abuse attempt to handle their anger:

> Most of us have received little help in learning to use our anger to clarify and strengthen ourselves and our relationships. Instead, our lessons have encouraged us to fear anger excessively, to deny it entirely, to displace it onto inappropriate targets, or to turn it against ourselves. We learn to deny that there is any cause for anger, to close our eyes to its true sources, or to vent anger ineffectively, in a manner that only maintains rather than challenges the status quo. Let us begin to unlearn these things so that we can use our "anger energy" in the service of our own dignity and growth. (p. 10)

Lerner asserts that anger is inevitable whenever a person is a victim, taken advantage of, manipulated or used, as occurs in acquaintance rape. As Lerner states, unfortunately, the way women often manage their anger is ineffective in the long run. These ineffective ways of managing anger include silent submission, ineffective fighting and blaming, and emotional distancing.

Lerner provides valuable advice for acquaintance rape survivors, although her book is not specifically addressed to that audience. She suggests that survivors ask themselves two questions. The first is: What unresolved and unaddressed issues with another person are getting played out in your current relationships? In the instance of acquaintance rape, the anger that a survivor directs at a mate, child, or boss may be anger that should be directed at the perpetrator rather than at these other targets. The second question is: How is the misdirected anger being maintained or kept alive? Additional important questions to consider are: Why do you persist in inappropriately expressing this anger at those around you instead of at the perpetrator? Are there payoffs in doing so?

A survivor writes that her promiscuity in the form of one-night stands related to the anger she felt toward men:

After the rape, I avoided any hint of sexuality. Then, as I started
dealing with my feelings, I began to have a series of one-night stands.
I did this not for intimacy, but out of anger and defiance. Sex was
cold. I trusted *no* men. At this point I went back into counseling to
deal with trust and anger. I realized I had to like and trust myself
before I could trust others.

The anger an acquaintance rape victim experiences may appear
in various problems-in-living. For example, Judi Hollis (1985) in *Fat
Is a Family Affair* describes the relationship between anger and eating
disorders. Hollis feels that people with eating disorders use food to
push down the anger within them that they are attempting to deny.
Eating is also fun and pleasurable, a temporary respite from feelings
of low self-esteem. On the outside the victim may smile ingratiat-
ingly and seem not at all angry, but in reality may be seething with
anger. In the eating process, the survivor may also withdraw from
other social contacts, in some instances, because of embarrassment
over her weight. A vicious cycle develops in which the survivor
shuts herself off from social contacts and uses food to gain pleasure
and solace.

Posttraumatic Stress Disorder

The impact of acquaintance rape on a victim may be seen from
the diagnostic perspective of posttraumatic stress disorder. Posttraumatic stress disorder is described in the *Diagnostic and Statistical
Manual of Mental Disorders* of the American Psychiatric Association
(1987) as follows:

The essential feature of this disorder is the development of characteristic symptoms following a psychologically distressing event that is
outside the range of usual human experience (that is, outside the
range of such common experiences as simple bereavement, chronic
illness, business losses, and marital conflict). The stressor producing
this syndrome would be markedly distressing to almost anyone, and
is usually experienced with intense fear, terror, and helplessness. The
characteristic symptoms involve reexperiencing the traumatic event,

avoidance of stimuli associated with the event or numbing of general responsiveness, and increased arousal. The diagnosis is not made if the disturbance lasts less than one month. (p. 247)

Various types of trauma may evoke posttraumatic stress disorder, including serious threats to a person's life or integrity, threats or harm done to family members or friends, sudden destruction of personal property or the community in which one resides, and witnessing someone being seriously injured or killed as a result of physical violence, an accident, a natural disaster or sexual assault.

Survivors of sexual assault by an acquaintance may attempt to push the original event out of their consciousness and try to forget it. They may reinforce this denial with alcohol or drugs. However, in posttraumatic stress disorder, the survivor involuntarily reexperiences the stressful event in various ways. For example, the survivor may have flashbacks and may experience dreams in which the event is relived.

Parallels can be drawn between the experiences of acquaintance rape survivors and Vietnam veterans. Both the acquaintance rape survivor and veteran complied with what was expected of them. For the veteran it was to kill; for the sexual assault survivor, it was to submit to the assault. Both were made to feel that what they were doing was expected of them, even though they may have been very resistant. The stress experienced by both in the situation in which they were placed was so severe that afterward they may have denied the events had occurred, the emotions associated with the event, or both (Patten, Gatz, Jones, & Thomas, 1989).

Some acquaintance rape survivors experience flashbacks of their sexual assault. Various stimuli may trigger a flashback, for example, smelling the shaving lotion worn by the acquaintance, being in the same location where the assault occurred, or engaging in consensual sex with a partner. To avoid the discomfort associated with these flashbacks, survivors may limit their contacts with others. Their fear of experiencing anxiety-provoking flashbacks, coupled with their inability to trust others and their fear of close relationships may force them to withdraw to themselves.

A survivor writes:

I am overly cautious in my relationships. Anybody who wears a mustache, I stay clear of (my assailant had a mustache). He also liked the musical group ZZ Top and now I can't stand hearing that music. I get the shakes—sort of like mild convulsions—when I start getting close to someone. Also, I get bouts of anxiety. The attacks are so bad that I get physically ill. After I really get to know someone, these symptoms start to get less and then fade away.

A survivor, raped by a fellow employee at the age of 20, describes her experience with posttraumatic stress disorder:

Immediately following the incident, for about 2 years, I had panic attacks during intercourse with another partner. I would feel suffocated and violated, even though I had consented to sexual activity.

Another survivor related that she left her marriage because of the effects the earlier sexual trauma had on her. She perceived her husband's desire for sex like those of the rapist "except without the force." Although she is a young woman, she does not date.

Another symptom of posttraumatic stress disorder that acquaintance rape survivors may exhibit is the absence of emotions that would be expected in someone who has experienced a stressful event. This effect is referred to as psychic numbing or emotional anesthesia. The psychically numbed person may feel detached or estranged from other persons and lose the ability to enjoy previously enjoyable activities. The numbness may be most pronounced in close relationships with other persons.

Duration of the Effects

How lasting are these effects that acquaintance rape survivors experienced? Survivors reported that years after their assault they still recall what happened, experience feelings of anger, and at times engage in self-blame. Although therapy has been helpful to many of the survivors, the effects of their intimate betrayal can never be entirely forgotten.

Researchers studied the long-term effects of acquaintance rape by comparing a group of survivors with a group of women who had not been sexually victimized. The researchers reported that although, on average, the sexual assault had occurred 15 years ago, there were still significant and substantial differences in the functioning of the sexual assault survivors and the nonvictims. The acquaintance rape survivors were 11 times more likely to be depressed, 6 times more likely to be severely fearful and anxious in social situations, and more than 2 times more likely to experience sexual dysfunctioning than their nonvictim counterparts. This shows the severity of the impact of acquaintance rape on those who experience such an assault (Kilpatrick, Best, Saunder, & Veronen, 1988).

Summary

Acquaintance rape takes a tremendous toll on its victims. The impact of this sexual assault is seen in the survivor's inability to trust others and their fear of intimacy. Also, survivors are left with intense feelings of anger toward their perpetrator that they may deny, project on other relationships in which they are involved, or suppress through the use of food, alcohol, or drugs. These problems may be seen in various areas of survivors' psychosocial functioning and may persist for years with varying degrees of intensity, unless the survivor receives help for these problems.

6 Marital Rape

Patricia Lynn Peacock

We were married. He wanted sex. I didn't and was forced.

My former husband was completely controlling. His threats and physical abuse gave him total control over me, including having sex long after he had destroyed any love or physical need that I felt for him.

He put the fear of God in me. I would have done anything not to be hurt by him again. It was like he owned me, like he took my soul and I had no rights. In a weird way he possessed me. I was helpless.

No matter who the people are or what their relationship is—the fault always lies with the person who *commits* the acts. Rape *is not* sex. Rape is power, aggression, domination, and always humiliation. It has to do with all things being unequal. It is a reminder of that. Letting one know for certain you have no choice in what's happening. It makes you feel less than human. Just like the family dog.

I felt lost afterward. I kept staring at him in disbelief as he slept. How could he injure someone and just fall asleep while I cried? I called my physician for help—someone I had known for years and trusted. He brushed me off. I felt humiliated.

Take each rapist, nail his penis to a wooden block in the middle of a
large field. Pour gasoline all over the block and around him. Hand
him a dull butter knife, flip a lit match, and let him make the choice—
cut it off or burn to death.

As we can sense from the quotations of some of the women who
responded to this research, the profound effects of marital rape are
extreme. The violent act of forcing one's spouse to engage in sexual
activity without consent destroys the most intimate and trusting
relationship of the marital bond. The physical, emotional, and economic scars caused by marital rape can be and often are long lasting
and can alter a victim's interpersonal relationships permanently.

This chapter was not initially planned to be a part of the book on
acquaintance rape. The research questionnaire was not designed to
examine marital rape in depth. Therefore, the information available
from the respondents raped by their spouse is more limited. However, their responses were so compelling, it was decided that this
form of acquaintance rape—marital rape—could not be ignored. It
is important that mental health workers, medical professionals,
social workers, attorneys, law enforcement personnel, clergy, and
elected officials realize that marital rape exists, and that it occurs
more often than we would like to realize.

The emergence of the long-hidden social problem of marital rape
into the forefront of widespread public awareness began in October
1978, when Greta Rideout was beaten and raped by her husband,
John. She filed charges against him under Oregon's recently revised
rape law, which rescinded the marital rape exemption (Augustine,
1991). Although the husband was acquitted by the courts, this Oregon
case received national coverage in the news and caused Americans
to begin to question antiquated laws that exempted a husband from
charges of raping his wife. As awareness has increased, the popular
media as well as scholarly articles and books have exposed the social
problem of marital rape.

As recently as June 1993, in Manassas, Virginia, Lorena Bobbitt
severed her husband's penis while he slept, claiming that he had
raped her and that as a result of the years of physical, sexual, and
emotional abuse she had suffered, this most recent rape caused her
to experience temporary insanity, and she assaulted him. Coverage

of this case has been international in scope. These cases represent extreme examples in the press, but do they represent anomalies in everyday reality for thousands of women? How often does rape within a marriage or cutting off a husband's penis occur? How many women have been raped by their husbands? Are there demographic differences in the nature, scope, and distribution of these acts of marital rape? These questions and more will be explored in this chapter.

Definition of Terms

For this chapter, *marital rape* will be defined as any sexual activity by a legal spouse that is performed or caused to be performed without the consent of the other spouse. These activities, as with acquaintance rape, include fondling, oral sex, anal sex, intercourse, or any other unwanted sexual activity. The commonly accepted legal definition of *rape* refers to sexual intercourse by a man with a woman, *not his wife*, without her consent (Augustine, 1991; Barshis, 1983; Bidwell & White, 1986; Freeman, 1985; Harman, 1984; Holtzman, 1986; Russell, 1982; Scheyett, 1988; Small & Tetreault, 1990). This definition actually denies the possibility of the occurrence of marital rape, and, because 40 women in the present research reported that in their minds they were raped by their spouses, it is not being used here. *Husband* is defined as the male spouse who is legally bound to his wife in marriage. *Wife* is defined as the female spouse who is legally bound to her husband in marriage. *Marriage* is defined as the legal union of a man and woman. In keeping with the terms employed elsewhere in this book, the terms *survivor* and *perpetrator* will be used to identify, respectively, those married women who have been sexually abused by a spouse and have succeeded or endured despite experiencing a serious trauma, and the husbands who committed the sexual assaults.

Of the 40 women who reported marital rape in the research questionnaire, 80% were forced to engage in nonconsensual sexual intercourse with their spouse, comparable to 82% of the respondents overall who reported being raped by an acquaintance. The married women, however, were more frequently forced to perform other sexual activities with their husband (such as oral and anal sex) compared

TABLE 6.1 Unwanted Sexual Behaviors That Married Survivors Were
Forced to Engage In

Behavior	Percentage [a]	(n)
Intercourse	88	(35)
Perpetrator fondling victim	48	(19)
Victim being forced to fondle perpetrator	45	(18)
Victim being forced to perform oral sex on perpetrator	45	(18)
Perpetrator performing oral sex on victim	17	(7)
Perpetrator engaging victim in anal sex	40	(16)

a. Percentages do not total 100% because survivors identified more than one behavior.

to those raped by acquaintances. (Refer to Table 1.1 for comparison
data.) Table 6.1 reports the sexual activities in which husbands
forced their wives to participate.

Having reviewed the definitions to be used in this chapter and
the forced sexual behaviors married survivors reported, it is of interest to briefly examine the legal history of rape in western civilization
to understand the omission of marital rape.

Legal History of the
Marital Rape Exemption

The basis of the legal history of the marital rape exemption is
found in 17th-century British common law (Augustine, 1991;
Barshis, 1983; Russell, 1982; Scheyett, 1988; Small & Tetreault, 1990).
Sir Matthew Hale (1609-1676), a British jurist, is credited with interpreting the English law for married women as grounds for exempt-
ing a husband from the charge of rape (Hale, 1736/1991; see also
Augustine, 1991; Freeman, 1985). He asserted that the implied or
irrevocable consent inherent in the marriage contract in which the
wife willingly gives herself to her husband negates the possibility
of marital rape. From the moment of marriage forward, the wife has
"given herself" to her husband, and may not refuse him any sexual
favor requested in the future. As an extension of implied consent,
and thereby the concept that whatever is desired in the marital

sexual relationship by the husband is his right, tradition protects the privacy of the marital relationship.

Another point of legal history involves the concept that the wife is chattel, or property of the husband. This point is based on the early English rape law that was enacted to protect the family of a proper-tied virgin should she be abducted and raped, which would result in the loss of the valuable property of the virgin. The penalties for such an offense were based on the equivalency of monetary damage to property, and thus a man could not be found guilty of defiling his own property (Scheyett, 1988).

Finally, Barshis (1983) presents the historical concept that because a man and woman are united into one legal body in marriage, a man could not be found guilty of raping himself. This concept was revoked by the passage of the Married Woman's Property Acts in the 1800s, when the identities of the husband and wife were legally separated.

There is a long history supporting the marital rape exemption. Since the early 1970s, with the growth of the feminist movement, laws regarding rape in general and marital rape in particular have come under attack, and there has been a national cry for reform (Coleman, 1978; Foster, 1977). In the United States, states have had to reevaluate their laws to confront the violent sexual victimization of women by their husbands.

Current Status of the
Marital Rape Exemption Law

Social concern, social awareness, and societal demand for action have resulted in important changes in the marital rape exemption laws in the United States since 1970, although Gelles (1977) found that in both his personal and professional experiences, marital rape is considered less serious than rape by a stranger or acquaintance. Consistent with Gelles are the findings of a survey by Jeffords (1984) in which he sought to determine sex role and religious views as variables affecting attitudes toward forced marital intercourse. He found that Judeo-Christian theology supports the ideology of the patriarchal society to the extent that the attitude concerning the severity of marital rape is mitigated. In further research, Jeffords and Dull (1982) also found that of 1,300 respondents in Texas to a questionnaire, 35% favored legal recourse for a woman raped by her spouse, whereas 65% did not believe a wife had the right to accuse her husband of rape.

In 1977, Oregon became the first state to repeal the marital rape exemption (Pagelow, 1992). Since that time, all states have examined their policies and laws governing the marital rape exemption. As of 1990, 48 states, plus the District of Columbia and federal lands in any state, hold that a husband can be prosecuted for raping his wife when he is living with her. The only two states in which marital rape is not a crime are North Carolina and Oklahoma. Of the 48 protective states, 20 have no exemption from prosecution, with every woman having equal protection. Each state defines marital rape differently, and variations of the exemption law may take many forms. For example, most states now recognize that marriage may not be a permanent state and therefore may except the exemption under certain signs of marital discord, such as separation (Small & Tetreault, 1990). Because each state's handling of marital exemption is different, whether through statutory or judicial means, it is important for persons who deal with victims and perpetrators of marital rape to be familiar with the laws pertaining to their respective state or territory.

Change does not come without costs and complications. The new laws have and will be challenged in courts as different interpretations are made. Definitions and the legal aspects of the concept of marital rape must be clarified and standardized (Augustine, 1991; Harman, 1984). Enforcement of the new laws, and the prosecution, conviction, and punishment of offenders also are necessary to establish credence to the intent and letter of the law and to publicly proclaim the legal abhorrence of marital rape. Guidelines for enforcement as well as suits for nonenforcement must be in place, with prevention ultimately the overall goal of any such social reform (Caringella-MacDonald, 1988). Violence against women in any and all forms must be eliminated. As with the recent international exposure of child sexual abuse, the active involvement of the media in exposing not only the widespread scope of this major social problem but also its short- and long-term effects will play a significant role in controlling or ameliorating the occurrence of marital rape.

Nature of Marital Rape

The social structure in the United States has been established on the historical concept of a patriarchy—a social structure that is defined by a hierarchy in which the male is strong, virile, and superior. The woman has been viewed as weak, inferior, and needing the protection, care, and attention of the male. Laws governing sex-related issues have traditionally supported the male perspective. As discussed earlier, the women's movement has forced a reexamination of this perspective; however, changes in the basic structure of society occur slowly.

The patriarchal family structure characterized by husband/father dominance represents one view of the nature of marital rape as representing the male/female difference with the dominance/submission dynamic at work overall (Boulding, 1978; Mackinnon, 1983). As one survivor states:

> I was brought up to believe that you do what your husband wants in the bedroom. He will be the teacher.

Another survivor writes:

> I thought for a long time I had not been a "good" wife/sex partner and that was why my husband felt he had to force me because I was not meeting *his* needs.

The traditional patriarchal family structure encourages the subjugation of women to men. A survey of 146 college men found that men characterized as "macho" were more accepting of marital rape than stranger rape, and that macho men were less opposed to sexual violence than their nonmacho counterparts (Sullivan & Mosher, 1990).

Brownmiller (1975) also supports the theory that marital rape is an extension of the patriarchal power structure and a part of the fundamentally larger spectrum of wife abuse. In perhaps the most extensive research to date on marital rape, Diana Russell (1982) urges that marital rape not be subsumed under the rubric of spouse abuse but be accorded attention to the enormity of the problem in its own sphere.

Another view of the nature of marital rape expresses the rape as an extreme act of power, domination, and control by a husband, not only on the body of the wife, but on her mind as well (Barshis, 1983; Gondolf, 1985; Holmstrom & Burgess, 1983). A survivor writes:

> I felt he would definitely hurt me physically if I didn't let this happen. I guess I didn't recognize there would be emotional scars. I would have much preferred physical scars because they go away much faster.

Power and control are characteristics of rape in general. The assault on the mind of a wife raped by her husband is also rape, as a survivor comments:

> He took my soul and I had no rights. In a weird way he possessed me.

Physical scars, however, are not to be ignored. In many cases, the nature of marital rape includes the presence of violence. Marital rape is more likely to occur in a marriage also characterized as physically violent (Bidwell & White, 1986; Frieze, 1983; Holtzman, 1986; Pagelow, 1992; Russell, 1982; Small & Tetreault, 1990). Hanneke, Shields, and McCall (1986) found that of 439 women in a combined sample of questionnaires and interviews on violence and women, only 8 cases of marital rape had occurred when not accompanied by some form of violence, and that 44.9% of those reporting battering also had been raped by their husband. Barshis (1983) reported that if a husband is violent toward his wife, he is more likely to be violent toward his children as well. Diana Russell (1982) found that there was a relationship between marital rape and battering. Of the 930 women surveyed for her research, only 4% admitted to rape without battering, 12% admitted battering only, and 10% reported both marital rape and battering. Koss et al. (1988) reported that of the 489 rape victims included in their study, acquaintance rapes were less violent than stranger rapes, but rapes by husbands or other family members were equally as violent as stranger rapes. Marital rape can be and often is accompanied by violence ranging from slapping,

TABLE 6.2 Types of Force Used by Perpetrators on Marital Rape Survivors

Type of Force	Percentage[a]	(n)
Verbal persuasion	63	(25)
Verbal threat	55	(22)
Physical intimidation	68	(27)
Drugged with alcohol or other drugs	5	(2)
Some physical roughness (slap or push)	50	(20)
Extreme physical roughness	28	(29)
Display of weapon	10	(4)
Injury with weapon	8	(3)
Other (not specified)	25	(10)

a. Percentages do not total 100% because survivors identified more than one type of force.

kicking, and being held down to bondage, the use of weapons, torture, and even death. Table 6.2 identifies the types of force used by the perpetrators against their wives in the marital rapes reported in the present research.

Although it was not possible to determine each form of force used by all of the perpetrators, some comments from the survivors are pertinent and illuminating.

> Often he would rape me while I was still sleeping in my bedroom. I would wake with him inside me. He wouldn't stop even after I asked him to.

> He would verbally abuse me while forcing my head down on him. He would say, "Come on, suck it, you bitch. You want me here."

> He just pulled me off the chair by my hair into the bedroom. He was telling me I deserved it.

Scope of Marital Rape

Researchers report an estimated 2 million instances of marital rape per year in the United States (Bidwell & White, 1986). Russell (1982) found in her research that marital rape is the most prevalent form of rape, outnumbering both stranger and acquaintance rape. In a sample of 930 women in the San Francisco area, she found that 14% of all women who had ever been married had been raped by their spouse at least once during the marriage with one third reporting 2 to 20 incidents, one third reporting more than 20 incidents, and one third reporting a one-time occurrence only. In the present survey, 40 of 278 or 14% of the sample reported incidents of marital rape with 34 of the 40 women (85%) reporting that they had been raped more than once by their spouse.

It is generally conceded that reported rapes represent only the tip of the iceberg in the actual number of incidents. With marital rape it can only be supposed that the reporting is even more limited. A clear definition of marital rape is not known to the general population, and many women feel that as a wife, they "owe" their husbands sex on demand (Frieze, 1983). Many more women, although forced to have sexual relations with their husbands, do not consider this as rape but as duty or marital obligation (Gelles, 1977).

Of the 40 women participating in the present research who reported marital rape, only 15 (38%) had knowledge of the terms *acquaintance rape* or *marital rape* prior to their own assaults, and only 12 (30%) defined their sexual assault as rape. The remaining 28 had responses similar to the following:

> I was married and thought I had to have intercourse whether I wanted to or not. I wanted him to get it over with so he would not be angry with me or the children.

> The rapes by my now ex-husband weren't considered rape in my mind at first because he was my husband at the time. I rationalized his behavior.

> At first I just wondered what I had done to cause it and what I could do to make him love me enough to be appealing to him in ways that he didn't need to hurt me to become aroused.

Whether through fear of not being believed, shame and guilt, or fear of retribution, most women who are raped by a spouse do not report the event(s) to authorities (Holtzman, 1986; Russell, 1982). In the present research, only 3 of the 40 women reported the rape(s) to the authorities, one had the rape reported by witnesses, and 3 prosecuted. One of the 3 survivors reporting states she was raped by her husband and 3 of his friends. She writes:

> I tried to report it, but the men were arrested on assault and battery charges only. The first question the police asked was why I didn't leave. When I told them they had tied me to a bed and had a gun and knives, they asked why I let them tie me up. None served any time.

Another survivor who reported her rape writes:

> I was told that the situation was a drunken domestic argument and things would be better after he sobered.

The third survivor who reported her rape describes what happened:

> I reported to the police the second time he raped me. By this time I knew that if I didn't report him and get him in jail, he would have come back again and that time I would have been dead. Or, I would have to flee the state with my daughter and run for the rest of my life.

Many women who indicated on the research questionnaire that they did not report the rape gave reasons for doing so. Following are some of their responses:

> I did not report because I felt no one would ever believe me. They would just think I did it and then got scared. That's what he told me. His family were police officers and he is one today.

> I didn't report because it was a family matter and for fear of his retaliation if I did report.

> I didn't report because I did not realize it was rape until 5 years later.

> Earlier I had reported my rape to church authorities who didn't believe me so why keep trying.

> I was too ashamed to report the rape. I felt responsible. I couldn't face friends and family if they knew.

Women raped by their husband who do tell someone face further victimization through humiliating treatment that compounds the horror of the original assault (Johnson, 1980). Only 6 (15%) of the 40 women reporting marital rape in the present research sought medical treatment following their rape. The woman who was raped by her husband and three of his friends was taken unconscious to the hospital where she remained for 6 weeks recovering from broken bones and internal injuries. This same woman wrote that when she prosecuted, she was "made to feel guilty." Another woman said that she was "treated with caution and with kindness and respect." Yet another reported:

> The medical examination was humiliating and devastating for me. I cried through the whole thing.

A woman raped by her husband sought medical treatment at a hospital where she was employed. She writes:

> I went to the hospital and had an examination. The medical examination was more embarrassing than reporting the rape. Another thing that made it bad was that I work at the same hospital and by the time I came back to work, quite a few of the people at work knew that I had been raped. The people in emergency, X ray, and medical records do not keep personal information to themselves.

One survivor was forced to have anal intercourse with her husband against her consent. She sought medical help from her family physician. She writes:

> I was so frightened of the anal intercourse and was physically injured —torn and bleeding. When my doctor minimized the trauma, I did not seek further treatment. I healed as best I could on my own.

These cases present alarming reports by the survivors of revictimization by those people they thought represented authority, care, concern, protection, and empathy. With an understanding that those who report or seek help because of marital rapes represent only a small percentage of the population actually experiencing this form of violation, it is vital that public policy change to accord the survivors the support necessary to avoid further similar occurrences.

Demographic Data
Regarding Marital Rape

Russell (1982) found that marital rape crossed all socioeconomic boundaries, ages, races, educational levels, and length of marriage. Russell also discovered that many women who were raped by their husbands had been married less than one year prior to the first incidence of marital rape. Yegidis (1988) reports this to be true as well; however, she found that of the 78 women in the Tampa Bay (Florida) area study who sought counseling for domestic difficulties, those reporting marital rape represented a lower socioeconomic group than the women not reporting marital rape. Frieze (1983) states that of the 137 women in her research sample who reported physical assault and marital rape, the wives who had several children, had never been employed prior to the marriage, and who had less education were more likely to be raped by their spouses.

Of the 40 women in the present research raped by their spouses, the average age at the time of the rape was 25. Marital rape, however, is not limited to young brides. In a study of 28 elderly women identified by protective service workers as possible abuse victims, 29% appeared to have been cases of marital rape (Ramsey-Klawsnik, 1991). In the present study, 33 (83%) of the 40 women were living with their perpetrators, having known these men from 2 months to 15 years. Some of the women reported that at the time of the first rape by their spouse, they were not married but later did marry the perpetrator. Of the 40 women, 29 (73%) were Caucasian, 9 (22%) were African American, and two were of other racial backgrounds. The majority of the respondents at the time of their rape were employed full-time and had some college education. The life situation of some of these survivors is summarized in the following comment of one survivor:

> I stayed with him for a while despite the rape in our marriage because I had no training for a job and had two babies in diapers. I always felt badly because I didn't leave sooner. After therapy, I came to realize it was a matter of survival.

Alcohol or drug usage by either the survivor or the perpetrator is often cited as a contributing factor in the incidence of marital rape, although certainly not an excuse for the violent behavior (Barnard, 1990; Frieze, 1983; Russell, 1982). In the present research, 37 of the 40 women raped by their spouses responded to the question inquiring if drugs or alcohol were being used at the time of the rape. Twenty (50%) reported their spouse had been using either drugs or alcohol or both at the time of the rape, and 30 (75%) of the survivors had been doing likewise. Of the women using alcohol or drugs, 23 (58%) blamed themselves for the rape because of their usage of substances. As one survivor wrote:

> He would get me high, then he would invite people over and use verbal and physical force to get me to do what he wanted me to do to him or others.

Bidwell and White (1986) discuss the role of marital rape in the family context. They contend that if there are children in a family where marital rape occurs, it may be safely assumed that the children are aware of at least the violence occurring in the marriage, if not even the rape itself. In the sample for the present research, several of the survivors reported their children were used as pawns in the rape. A survivor writes:

> I just let him rape me. He said he was going to get my daughter if I didn't let him. I felt it was my only alternative and it makes me feel like shit.

Another survivor writes:

> I needed to keep my faculties to protect myself and my children.

Survivors' History of Prior Abuse

It is not uncommon for acquaintance rape survivors to have been survivors of earlier forms of abuse, including physical, emotional, and/or sexual abuse. Russell (1982) reported that 68% of incest victims were victims of rape or attempted rape by a nonrelative compared to 38% of nonincest survivors. Also, almost three times as

TABLE 6.3 Marital Rape Survivors' History of Prior Childhood Abuse

Form of Abuse	Percentage[a]	(n)
Emotional	68	(27)
Physical	35	(14)
Sexual	53	(21)
Not at all	18	(7)

a. Percentages do not total 100% because survivors identified more than one type of abuse.

many incest survivors had been raped by their husbands compared to women who had not been sexually abused in their childhood. In the present research, survivors were asked to identify childhood incidence of abuse by a family member. Table 6.3 reports the prior history of childhood abuse for survivors in this research.

Comments made by these survivors reveal their previous experience with abuse.

> I was afraid to seek help immediately at first. I was molested by a family member as a child and then was abused for telling. I was scared to report my husband when he raped me and our daughters.

Another survivor writes of her inability to view marital rape as rape:

> I have numbed myself for many years during sex due to things in my childhood such as physical, emotional, and sexual abuse by a grandfather and uncle. After I finally learned I was not at fault and quit blaming myself, I hated all men.

One survivor describes both incestuous and marital rape experiences:

> My stepfather's favorite and most used threats were made against my mother and siblings. I remember on one occasion I refused to perform oral sex on him and he threatened that on the next day he would beat my brother. I remained adamant and on the following day he beat my brother. I called the police for the abuse against my brother. They refused to do anything. He never again tried to force me to perform

oral sex though. My husband forced me to do oral sex as well as
intercourse and anal sex.

Finally, a survivor writes:

> I cannot separate the rape by my husband from the incest I experi-
> enced as a child as far as trust and intimacy are concerned. I don't
> believe I ever would have been involved with this man had I not
> been sexually molested as a child.

Effects of Marital Rape

The effects of marital rape on the survivors have been studied in
some depth considering the brief time the problem has been recognized and reported. These effects include physical trauma to intense
psychological consequences, harming the survivors in ways far
beyond the scope of observable scars (Scheyett, 1988). Russell (1982)
reported that in her sample of 930 women, 52% of the women raped
by a spouse indicated that the rape(s) had long-term effects on their
lives compared to 25% raped by an acquaintance and 39% raped by
strangers.

A survivor in the present research of marital rape survivors
writes:

> When a woman is raped by an acquaintance, it's hard to report
> because you know you have to deal with this person again. Also,
> you likely know others who know and possibly like him. In the case
> of marital rape, it's most difficult because you have to live with your
> assailant day after day and they may have major control over your
> life. In my opinion, although somewhat biased, I believe marital rape
> is the hardest to deal with, and after 2 years away from him I remain
> afraid and celibate.

Included in the long-term effects of marital rape, women have
reported negative feelings toward men; low self-esteem; feelings of
fear, anxiety, guilt, embarrassment, and outrage; changes in behaviors, including an increase in drinking and a refusal to consider

remarriage; and depression (Bidwell & White, 1986; Frieze, 1983; Russell, 1982).

In the present study, the research questionnaire asked the marital rape survivors how their rape by a spouse affected their intimacy and ability to trust. Following are some survivors' comments:

I did not date for 5 years.

I don't trust men hardly at all now.

The total pattern of abuse, emotional and sexual, has made me mistrusting and very leery of men and relationships with men.

It is very difficult to trust in anyone, especially men, because of my rape. I find myself hypervigilant when it comes to my current relationships.

I do not trust people in general anymore. Intimacy is definitely a problem. I hate to do something when I'm told that I'm married and its my job. Maybe I want too much.

I feel worthless and I also feel the only thing I have to give to a relationship is sex.

Marital rape not only affects the individuals involved, but children, too, can and are affected by this violence in the home. Children exposed to emotional trauma often learn the patterns of violence, including sexual violence, and replicate this violence while still young and through their adult lives. Thus, violence becomes an intergenerational pattern (Barshis, 1983). The family unit also is jeopardized as a result of marital rape. Although the research questionnaire did not directly address the outcome of the marital rape survivors' marriages, many women commented on this issue as follows:

I'm divorced now.

For 5 to 6 years at least, I hated my husband and he used coercion to keep me in the relationship.

I married two more times after the rape by my first husband but have been divorced for 12 years and probably never will remarry or get into a long-term relationship.

I am separated at the moment and I feel very much alone. I think the rape has contributed to the separation. I feel sometimes like I'm bad because this happened to me and I probably deserve to be treated like I am nothing/no one.

My second husband had to pay for the "sins" of my first, sexually abusive husband.

For these women and thousands like them, counseling is one form of help. In the present research, 36 (90%) women revealed the occurrence of their marital rape to someone, and 26 (65%) of the women sought some form of counseling. Many of the women sought help from a rape crisis center; however, these data must be interpreted in the light of the fact that the research questionnaires were sent to rape crisis centers where these survivors were seeking help. Unfortunately, many marital rape survivors do not seek help after their sexual victimization by their mates.

Russell (1982) suggests that mental health professionals should assume marital rape occurs for all women who are in marriages in which violence is involved. She also found that most women who have been sexually abused as children become victims of rape in adulthood. With appropriate counseling, however, this chain of violence can be broken.

Warning Signs

The women in this survey volunteered information that they thought would help other women recognize warning signs in men who have the potential to rape. Their comments included the following: Their husband showed an extreme interest in and use of pornography, used alcohol to excess, and often used sex as a pay-off in the marital relationship. Survivors also shared their concern about their husbands' difficulty in handling anger. Anger and the need to control their spouse and children were a focal issue in the marriages in which marital rape occurred. Although these issues may also be seen in marriages where husbands do not rape their wives, these are important signals of which mental health professionals should be aware as they counsel couples.

Summary

This chapter has focused on a specific type of acquaintance rape —namely, rape by a spouse. A historical perspective on this social problem has been presented. Marital rape survivors have shared their comments regarding how their rape occurred and the impact this assault has had on their lives.

One survivor provided a beautiful summation for this chapter on marital rape by writing:

> Marital rape is just not discussed enough so that people can be comfortable talking about it. The public needs to know that rape *can* occur in a marriage. How can we begin to change the assumption that being a wife does not mean being the property of the husband? Marital rape is so intermingled with this issue that the only hope I see is younger women getting educated early that they have sole control of their bodies. Rape in general is seen too many times as partly or entirely the fault of the woman. This assumption has to be changed. People must know that rape can and does happen even in marriages. It's OK to talk about it, to report it, to prosecute.

I'm careful whom I tell about my boy-friend raping me because most people just don't understand.

—An acquaintance rape survivor

7 Understanding Acquaintance Rape

Why would someone rape an acquaintance? How can we understand this problem? What factors are associated with acquaintance rape? This chapter will answer these questions by focusing on (a) common myths about acquaintance rape and (b) theoretical perspectives based on research for understanding acquaintance rape. A knowledge of commonly held myths about acquaintance rape, as well as theoretical perspectives for understanding this social problem, is important to your work of helping survivors in their recovery and in your efforts to prevent the problem from occurring.

Common Myths About Acquaintance Rape

Prior to discussing theoretical perspectives for understanding acquaintance rape, we must examine commonly held myths about this social problem. For the purposes of this book, we define *myths* as delusions or misunderstandings that a large number of people hold about acquaintance rape. Being aware of acquaintance rape myths is important because these myths affect the way society deals with this social problem and the manner in which survivors attempt to cope with their victimization. Several myths will be identified.

Myth 1: The Victim Is Responsible

When a problem occurs in human behavior that we do not understand, there is a tendency to hold the victim responsible. In other words, we blame the victim. Recall how frequently you have heard comments that blame the victim when acquaintance rape occurs. "Why did she invite him to her apartment?" "Was she drinking?" "What did she do to lead him on?" Behind all of these questions is the assumption that it was the victim's behavior that caused the sexual assault. The victim is blamed for what happened. Little or no mention is made of the perpetrator and his responsibility for the crime that he committed.

The commonly held myth that the victim is responsible is reflected in the way some acquaintance rape survivors handle their own victimization—namely, they blame themselves for what happened. We have seen many examples of survivors blaming themselves for their sexual assault in their comments in previous chapters. Survivors often express self-blame in the form of "if only" or "should" statements. "If only I hadn't gone to his apartment to listen to records." "If only I had not been so trusting." "I should never have gone out with him."

Following are some examples of self-blame and "should" statements from our research participants. A young woman was raped by the maintenance man in the apartment complex where she lived. The man appeared at her apartment after she reported a leaking faucet to management. Later, reflecting back on her rape by the maintenance man, she comments:

> I felt I should not have let him come in—that I should have been able to make him leave. I felt to blame because I was stupid and let him come in.

Another survivor, thinking back on her rape by a boyfriend, describes him as being very possessive of her. He did not want to share her with others when they were out in public. As she looks back on his behavior, she engages in self-blame:

> In retrospect, . . . I feel so foolish for not seeing this behavior as being indicative of extreme controlling behavior. I should have seen that.

Frequently survivors engage in retrospective thinking after their rape and use this knowledge in a self-blaming manner. Some mental health therapists refer to this as "stinkin' thinkin' "—an absence of reality in how the victim perceives what happened. The survivor engages in a process of comparing what should have happened with what actually occurred, ignoring circumstances of which the survivor may now be aware, but was not aware at the time of the sexual assault. The end result is the survivor unrealistically assumes blame for what occurred.

So pervasive is the victim-blaming response from the victims, her significant others, and from the general public, that we must wonder what it is in human nature that causes us to hold victims responsible for their suffering at the hands of others. Several explanations may be given.

Ronnie Janoff-Bulman (1992) in her book *Shattered Assumptions* states that human beings want to assume that we live in an orderly world and that we can expect to be protected from misfortune. She cites the following internal dialogue that often goes on in the mind of the victim that reflects a sense of invulnerability based on this false assumption.

> My world is benevolent. Even in such a good world negative events happen, even if relatively infrequently. Yet when they occur they are not random, but rather meaningfully distributed. They happen to people who deserve them, either because of who they are or what they did or failed to do. I am a good, competent, careful person. Bad things couldn't happen to me: (p. 19)

People tend to overestimate the likelihood of positive events and underestimate the likelihood of negative events happening to them. Janoff-Bulman (1992) identifies this as the "illusion of invulnerability" (p. 19). Thus, when bad things (such as rape) do happen to us or to someone else, our initial response is to try to make sense of the event by blaming. If we blame the victim, the bad thing either never happened, or, if it did happen, it was the victim's (who probably deserved it) fault. Little wonder then that frequently victims blame themselves, perpetrators are absolved of responsibility for their behavior, family members are not supportive, and the legal system fails to respond with justice. Rather, to hold the perpetrator responsible for the rape is to accept the reality of the event and to thus accept that bad things do in fact happen and some persons are at times unjustly victimized.

Myth 2: Women Say "No" but Really Mean "Yes"

Another commonly held myth regarding acquaintance rape implies that women want to engage in sexual activities with men but must pretend they are not interested. This myth suggests that traditional roles for males and females prescribe that men must be aggressive in their interpersonal relationships with women and that women in turn must be passive. Included in this passive or "feminine" role is a denial of interest in sex that supposedly is opposite to how women actually feel about sex. Thus, although women will say "No" to sexually aggressive behavior from men, they are merely playing out their passive role, and actually mean "Yes." Therefore, a woman's response of "No" is interpreted as license to pursue her even more aggressively. A T-shirt for sale at Venice Beach, California, graphically portrays this acquaintance rape myth. Printed across the front of the T-shirt is the following inscription, "What part of NO don't you understand?"

Research shows that males and females who hold traditional stereotypical views about male/female relationships engage in more victim blame than their counterparts who do not subscribe to these views. Individuals subscribing to rigid prescriptions for how males and females should behave, such as that males are expected to be aggressive and females to act passive, also tend to excuse males' sexually aggressive behavior as appropriate (Bernard, Bernard, & Bernard, 1985; Brownmiller, 1975; Burt, 1983; Collier & Resick, 1987; Dull & Giacopassi, 1987; Jenkins & Dambrot, 1987; Margolin, Miller,

& Moran, 1989; Muehlenhard & Linton, 1987; Russell, 1975; Shotland & Goldstein, 1983).

Based on the myth that women do not speak honestly and openly about their sexual intent, men frequently misperceive cues from their female partners. Research focusing on differences in the way men and women perceive each other found that males rated females in photographs as more sexy and seductive than did their female counterparts. Also, men rated women wearing revealing clothing as more sexy and seductive than did women rating the same photographs (Abbey, Cozzarelli, McLaughlin, & Harnish, 1987). Research also shows that men tend to view the world from a more sexual perspective than do women and are more likely to interpret women's friendliness as seductiveness (Abbey, 1982). In studies involving samples of male and female college students viewing scenarios of two individuals on a date, no matter who initiated the date, who paid, or where the couple went, men were always more likely than women to interpret the behavior as a sign that the women wanted sex (Muehlenhard, 1988; Muehlenhard et al., 1985). Based on studies such as these, the conclusion may be made that many awkward moments may occur in dating relationships where intentions need to be clarified. Men may interpret a cue, such as how their date is dressed or behaves, as implying sexual availability when the date did not intend to give this message. These misperceptions may eventually result in sexually aggressive behavior on the part of the male.

Myth 3: Women Can Always
Say "No" or Resist Forced Sex

This myth represents a double bind for women in their relationships with men. The myth asserts that in sexual situations women are expected to be cooperative as well as in control of the outcome (Parrot, 1988b). Women are socialized from childhood to be accommodating to men, eager to please, and protective of the male ego. Acting in a relationship with a man in this manner may not present a serious problem until the woman is in a high-risk situation, such as when she is being forced to engage in sex against her will. She is then expected to be resistant, to defend herself, and to fight off her aggressor. If she becomes assertive and firm in her resistance to sexual activity, in addition to being physically overpowered she is accused of being "unfeminine," a "tease," or a "bitch." A woman will find it difficult to defend herself against such treatment. She typically doubts and second guesses herself when she is not exhibiting the expected passive, compliant, stereotypical feminine behavior.

One young woman voiced what is frequently heard by counselors when a woman has submitted, but not consented to, sexual activity:

> He was always so nice when we were with our friends—for instance, at parties. I thought he liked me, and I liked having someone interested in me. The first time we were alone together he became very aggressive. He said he knew what I wanted, and then he forced himself on me. I didn't want sex. I just wanted to be with him and have him like me. I didn't feel like I could say "No" because I could see how angry he would get. I was afraid of his anger.

Myth 4: Once Men Are Sexually Aroused, Sex Is Inevitable

This myth assumes that there is a point of no return for men once physiological arousal occurs. Although sexual arousal may be a precursor to acquaintance rape, the way men cognitively handle their sexual arousal determines the outcome of their behavior. Men are able to control their behavior, including behaviors associated with sexual arousal. Several factors affect the way a man responds to sexual arousal, as we shall see later, including the extent to which sex is premeditated and a male's use of alcohol.

Personifying the penis by giving it humorous names represents one way men play out the myth that they cannot control their sexual arousal. It is as if their penis operates independently of them. The expression sometimes is heard, "The little head thinks for the big head." This statement, although "humorously" made, supports the myth that a man cannot always be expected to control his sexual desires. Naming the penis, as occurred in the movie *Peggy Sue Got Married*, as "Lucky Chuckie" or other names implies a separation of this body organ from the rest of the body and that the penis operates independently from the man's cognitive functions. Naming the penis also reinforces the myth that a male can be expected to have difficulty controlling his sexual organ. This myth in turn covertly shifts responsibility away from the perpetrator when sexual assault occurs (Parrot, 1988b).

Single-Factor
Theoretical Explanations

Three theoretical approaches for understanding rape will now be presented that focus primarily on a single factor. These theories have varying degrees of support from research. They are the feminist, social learning, and evolutionary theories of rape.

Feminist Theory

The feminist theory of rape asserts that rape is the result of male domination and exploitation of women. Inequality exists between the genders in society. This can be seen, for example, in the economic and political arenas where men dominate in commerce and in the formulation of public policy. Rather than equality of status existing between males and females in society, women, in many instances, may be described as relatively powerless.

Feminist theory asserts that this powerlessness not only influences relationships between the genders in corporate boardrooms, in legislatures, and other societal institutions, but also in the interpersonal relationships between the sexes. As men feel they must dominate and control women in the world of commerce, so feminist theory states that men feel they must dominate and control women in their interpersonal relationships, including their sexual relationships. The resultant effect is that some men will engage in sexually aggressive acts against women as part of their need to dominate and control (Ellis, 1989). Thus, the feminist perspective views rape as not primarily a sexual act but rather a crime of violence and humiliation. The victim experiences an overwhelming fear for her existence and a deep sense of powerlessness and helplessness (Gise & Paddison, 1988).[1]

Social Learning Theory

This theory suggests that repeated exposure to violence tends to desensitize individuals to inherent dangers in aggressive behavior and may even create in persons a desire to engage in such behavior. Social learning theory suggests that we are receiving constant exposure to violence, including violence occurring in the context of the sexual relationship. Women are often the object of this violence as seen in movies, television, and especially pornographic videos. The constant exposure to violence, especially sexual violence, in the mass media may make viewers callous or unaware of its effect on the victim—humiliation, suffering, fear—consequences that can affect the victim for life. Although television alone cannot be blamed for this, this media form has graphically brought violence into the home of very person.

Evolutionary Theory

The evolutionary theory suggests that males and females experience the reproductive process differently based on the evolution of the species. Males show greater concern with mating compared to females who must devote time and energy to the gestation and care of children. According to Ellis (1989):

Basically, evolutionary theorists consider aggressive copulatory tactics as an extreme response to natural selection pressure for males to be generally more assertive than females in their attempts to copulate. However, because forced copulations reduce the ability of females to confine coitus primarily to males who will help care for offspring that they produce, females should have evolved strong tendencies to avoid, resist forced copulation, or both. According to evolutionary theorists, the resulting tension between the different optimal approaches to reproduction for males and females is responsible for much of the frustration, compromise, and deception both sexes exhibit during courtship (and, to a lesser degree, throughout life).

In summary, the evolutionary theory of rape considers sexual assault as resulting from natural selection for males who are eager to copulate with numerous sex partners, and females who are strongly committed to retaining major control over who will mate with them. The natural selection pressure for this sex difference largely emanates from the fact that males can produce offspring (in potentially large numbers) without gestating them, whereas females cannot. Any genes that happen to incline males to rape, therefore, could become quite prevalent in a mammalian population, except to the degree that fairly effective "counterstrategies" (from females or their relatives) were to also evolve. (pp. 15-16)

The evolutionary theory of rape differs from the feminist theory in that the latter emphasizes a desire for males as a group to maintain control or supremacy over females as a group. Evolutionary theory views sexual motivation largely in terms of individual males wishing to possess and control individual females for sexual purposes (Ellis, 1989).

Two Integrative Models for Understanding Acquaintance Rape

Two theoretical perspectives or models that integrate factors from previously discussed theories will be presented. They are the five-part model and the multivariate model.

Five-Part Model

This model places primary responsibility for acquaintance rape with the male. The model involves five parts:

- Physiological sexual arousal
- Cognitions that justify sexual aggression
- The emotional state of the aggressor
- Personality problems of the aggressor
- Situational factors

These components may be viewed as factors associated with the possibility of sexually aggressive behavior occurring in interpersonal relationships between males and females.

Physiological Sexual Arousal. Sexual arousal is a physiological phenomenon that underlies socially appropriate or inappropriate sexual behavior. Physiological arousal per se, however, is not the sole basis for sexual aggression in all cases. Rather, the male must think about the sexual arousal he is experiencing before he acts on this stimulus (Hall & Hirschman, 1991).

Cognitions That Justify Sexual Aggression. The way in which a male thinks about or processes in his mind the sexual arousal he is experiencing is important to how he eventually acts. He may make an accurate or inaccurate appraisal of what he is physically experiencing. For example, he may accurately appraise the situation as one in which his acquaintance does not want to engage in sexual activity and he therefore stops pursuing such activity. His thinking or appraisal of the situation, on the other hand, may be inaccurate. For example, he may be influenced by an inappropriate belief system regarding male/female roles or he may subscribe to certain rape myths discussed earlier and act on his sexual arousal despite his acquaintance's nonconsent. Another option is that he may simply chose to ignore moral or ethical reasons for controlling his sexually aggressive behavior. Finally, the use of drugs or alcohol may interfere with his ability to accurately appraise the situation or may break down inhibitions with the result being that he follows through on acting out the sexual arousal he is experiencing (Hall & Hirschman, 1991).

Emotional State. The male's emotional state may also affect this thinking process when experiencing sexual arousal. He may have anger or hostility toward women based on earlier life experiences or interpersonal relationships. These feelings may be so intense and overwhelming that they break down his normal inhibitions against sexually aggressive behavior and consequently he may proceed to act on his sexual arousal (Hall & Hirschman, 1991).

Personality Problems. A man's earlier life experiences such as parental divorce, parental neglect, or physical, emotional, or sexual abuse may create personality problems that increase his likelihood of engaging in sexually aggressive behavior. Other socialization or developmental factors, such as his level of education, occupational status, and social skills in interpersonal relationships, may relate to his inability to inhibit a tendency to engage in sexually aggressive behavior (Hall & Hirschman, 1991).

Situational Factors. Finally, situational factors may increase the likelihood of a male sexually aggressing following sexual arousal. Studies on differences between women who successfully resisted being sexually victimized and those who did not identify important situational variables associated with acquaintance rape. For example, sexual assault was more likely to occur when the man and woman were in a socially isolated area, where previous sexual intimacy had occurred, where unclear statements of nonconsent were made, where drugs or alcohol were being used by one or both parties, or where peer support was present such as occurs in gang rapes (Amir, 1971; Hall & Hirschman, 1991; Koss, 1985; Koss et al., 1988). Also, men may be more likely to engage in sexually abusive behavior if they have experienced physical or sexual abuse as children (Baldwin & Oliver, 1975; Bernard & Bernard, 1983; Conger, Burgess, & Barrett, 1979; Elmer, 1950; Green, Gaines, & Sandgrund, 1974; Johnson & Morse, 1968; Kaufman & Zigler, 1987; Nurse, 1964; Oliver & Taylor, 1971; Paulson & Chaleff, 1973; Selkin, 1979; Silver, Dublin, & Lourie, 1969; Smith & Williams, 1992; Wiehe, 1992). Women sexually abused as children may be at greater risk for sexual victimization in adulthood in part due to their poor self-esteem (Falaler, 1989; Herman & Hirschman, 1977; McGuire & Wagner, 1978; Summit & Kryso, 1978; Tasi, Feldman-Summers, & Edgar, 1979; Wiehe, 1990).

Multivariate Model

The multivariate model identifies variables related to the likelihood or possibility that a male might commit sexual assault (Berkowitz, 1992). These variables can also be used to identify individuals at risk for committing sexual assault. All of the variables comprising the model, however, need not be present for sexual assault to occur. This model includes the following variables:

- Perpetrator characteristics
- Situational factors associated with acquaintance rape
- The extent to which the perpetrator misperceives the sexual intents of his partner
- Characteristics associated with the woman's increased risk of sexual victimization

Figure 7.1 shows the causal relationships among these variables. Each will be briefly described.

The perpetrator's socialization experiences, beliefs, and attitudes toward sexuality may reflect themes of control and power over women, acting tough and unemotional, and getting one's sexual needs met without concern for one's sexual partner. Rape-supportive myths, discussed earlier in this chapter, may further reinforce these socialization patterns. The victim's socialization may complement the male's in that she may assume a passive, nonassertive role thereby allowing him to play the role of aggressor.

Personality characteristics of perpetrators such as early and frequent childhood sexual experiences (forced and voluntary), aggressive attitudes toward women, and a need to dominate a sexual partner may serve as preconditions for perpetrating sexual aggression in acquaintance relationships.

Situational variables may also be a significant factor. These include the use of drugs and alcohol by the perpetrator or victim, meeting in isolated areas, and the man paying for all the expenses of the date—thereby setting a climate of obligation for the female to comply with his sexual demands.

The perpetrator may misperceive his acquaintance's sexual intent. The way in which an acquaintance is dressed, interpersonal distance between the perpetrator and acquaintance, and eye contact may be misperceived by the male as cues indicating sexual interest and intent on the part of his female partner (Muehlenhard, 1987). Depending on the interaction of the variables, sexual assault may or may not occur.

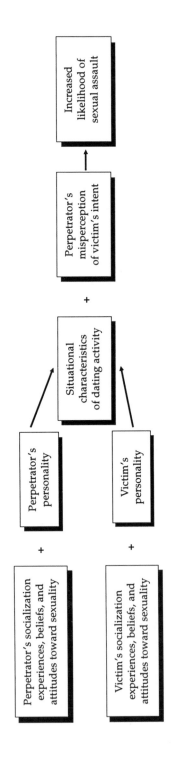

Figure 7.1. An Integrative Model of Sexual Assault and Acquaintance Rape

SOURCE: Berkowitz, A. (1992). In *Journal of American College Health, 40*(1). pp. 175-180. Reprinted with permission of the Helen Dwight Reid Educational Foundation. Published by Heldref Publications, 1319 Eighteenth St., N.W., Washington, DC 20036-1802. Copyright © 1992.

Summary

Various myths and theoretical perspectives for understanding acquaintance rape have been presented. How do these myths and theoretical perspectives help us to understand the phenomenon of acquaintance rape? First, we must state that our knowledge about this social problem is still developing. Acquaintance rape has only been studied by researchers for the past several decades. As acquaintance rape becomes more widely acknowledged and survivors are willing to identify themselves as victims, more research can occur and further understanding of the problem will result.

The research data suggest that acquaintance rape is a complex problem. Acquaintance rape must be viewed from various perspectives—biological, psychological, social, and cultural. When we approach acquaintance rape from a theoretical perspective, taking into account also the affect of the commonly held myths, clues for intervening and preventing this social problem begin to appear, the focus of subsequent chapters.

Note

1. We are aware of divergencies in current feminist thinking. Some contemporary feminists recognize that male sexuality can be violent but argue that the sexual freedom acquired by women entails risks and that, instead of insisting that men be less aggressive, women must be prepared to accept responsibility for their own safety and for sexual behavior that may put them at risk to rape (see Kaminer, 1993). We believe, however, that such a "neo-feminist" point of view discounts the experience of large numbers of women who have suffered the painful consequences of male aggression, and it relieves men of their responsibility to engage in sexual relationships that are mutually respectful and consensual.

My friends warned me against going to
court against the guy who raped me. My
assailant's attorney attacking what I said
made me feel like I was being raped again.
—An acquaintance rape survivor

8 The Legal Aspects of Acquaintance Rape

Gary W. Paquin

The Crime of Rape

The complexity of acquaintance rape is nowhere more evident than in the judicial arena where attempts to prosecute the offender and execute justice for the victim depend on proving the absence of consent to sexual activity. Under common law, rape is considered an act of sexual intercourse by a man with a woman who is not his wife by force and against her will. In situations where the woman is not able to consent, intercourse in generally held to be against her will.[1] Situations where the woman cannot consent would include where she is incompetent, drugged by the perpetrator, or underage. Although consent is the primary issue of fact that the court must decide, particularly in acquaintance rape cases where intercourse and identity of the male are being admitted to, feminist scholars have been quick to point out that it has been a woman's freedom to choose sexual partners that has not been protected by the law. Rather, her "virtue" or chastity has been regarded as the property right of fathers and husbands (Bessmer, 1976). In many ways the victim's character is as much at issue as the actions of the rapist, despite recent efforts to protect victims from such scrutiny through rape shield laws.

This chapter will examine the law of rape in general, the emergence of the crime of marital rape, the unique legal problems surrounding nonstranger rape, and the criminal process of such cases, as well as the use of civil and other noncriminal remedies to this social problem. The emphasis in the last part of this chapter will focus on how human service professionals can assist victims in this process.

Rape From a Legal Perspective

A brief review of traditional rape law will be given to provide the climate and challenges you will face when working with acquaintance rape survivors, especially when survivors attempt to seek redress from the courts for their assault.

The common law definition of rape was given earlier. Acquaintance rape is generally understood to be nonconsensual sex that does not involve physical injury or explicit threat of physical injury (Pineau, 1989). As has been discussed in earlier chapters, the nature of the relationship between the parties in an acquaintance rape can vary from having been sexually intimate previously to simply knowing each other through where they work, live, or attend school. To increase very low conviction rates, in some states rape is called sexual assault to emphasize the power and control issues of the attack rather than the sexual component. Some writers question minimizing the highly humiliating and embarrassing nature of the act by de-emphasizing its sexual nature (Estrich, 1987). There is little indication, however, that the change has led to increased conviction rates (Marsh, Geist, & Caplan, 1987).

There are several ways in which rape can occur: (a) rape by force or violence, (b) rape by threat and fear, and (c) rape with an unconscious or incompetent woman (Bessmer, 1976). In rape by force or violence, the force by the attacker must be sufficient to overcome the resistance by the woman. Also, the resistance must be present in an intensity relative to the circumstances of the rape. The second category, rape by threat and fear, requires a situation where any resistance would be physically dangerous or futile. Typically, these cases involve the brandishing of a deadly weapon or the presence of several attackers.

A legislative example of these two categories can be seen in the *California Penal Code:*

> a. An act of sexual intercourse with a person not the spouse of the perpetrator, under any of the following circumstances:
>
> 2. Where it is accomplished against a person's will by means of force, violence, duress, menace, or fear of immediate and unlawful bodily injury on the person of another.
>
> 6. Where the act is accomplished against the victim's will by threatening to retaliate in the future against the victim or any other person, and there is a reasonable possibility that the perpetrator will execute the threat. As used in this paragraph "threatening to retaliate" means a threat to kidnap or falsely imprison, or to inflict extreme pain, serious bodily injury or death.
>
> b. As used in this section, "duress" means a direct or implied threat of force, violence, danger, hardship, or retribution sufficient to coerce a reasonable person of ordinary susceptibilities to perform an act that would have otherwise not been performed, or acquiesce in an act to which one otherwise would not have submitted. The total circumstances, including age of victim, and his or her relationship to defendant are factors to consider in appraising existence of duress.
>
> c. Menace means any threat, declaration, or act that shows an intention to inflict an injury upon another. (*California Penal Code,* 1991)

The examination of reasonable fear is a carryover from the old common law version of rape and is part and parcel of the myths about vindictive or spurned women who cry rape. The Biblical account of Potiphar's wife is often cited as an example. Potiphar's wife tempted Joseph but he spurned her. Consequently, she had him thrown into prison for attempting to seduce her. Hence, the following comment of Lord Chief Justice Hale is often quoted: "It is an accusation easily to be made, and hard to be proved, and harder to be defended by the party accused tho never so innocent" (Hale, 1991, p. 635). Given the myth that women are not trustworthy, as reflected in the above comment, some evidence of struggle on the part of the woman was necessary for rape to be found.

This attitude has been carried over into the 20th century as evidenced by the other often quoted work of one of this country's most influential scholars in the area of evidence. Wigmore (1971) strongly recommends that women be subjected to a psychiatric evaluation before being allowed to testify in rape trials:

Modern psychiatrists have amply studied the behavior of errant young girls and women coming before the courts in all sorts of cases. Their psychic complexes are multifarious, distorted partly by diseased derangements or abnormal instincts, partly by bad social environment, partly by temporary physiological or emotional conditions. One form taken by these complexes is that of contriving false charges of sexual offenses. (p. 736)

As this quotation reflects, due to pseudoscience or the misinterpretation of psychiatric insights, women who file rape complaints are no longer likely to be considered evil but rather just crazy.

The third and last type of rape is rape with an unconscious or incompetent woman. A typical legislative example of this category can again be seen in the *California Penal Code:*

3. Where a person is prevented from resisting by any intoxicating or anesthetic substance, or controlled substance, administered by or with the privity of the accused.

4. Where a person is at the time unconscious of the nature of the act, and this is known to the accused. (*California Penal Code,* 1991)

It is important to note that where a victim is intoxicated, unless she is unconscious or alcohol/drugs are pushed on her by the rapist, she has little protection against someone who takes advantage of her intoxicated state when it is self-induced. In fact, the victim of acquaintance rape who is intoxicated will more likely be seen as precipitating the rape as a result of her intoxication. Research shows that police are likely to define a complaint as unfounded based on a pattern of alcohol or drug use (Kerstetter, 1990).

There are other categories of rape such as statutory rape (sex with a child typically by an adult) and rape by fraud. In these cases, consent may have been given but the female is assumed not to be capable of valid consent. Depending on the state, in statutory rape cases perpetrators may give as a defense either "a reasonable mistake of fact" of the girl's age or sexual experience. An old statutory rape case provided one of the hallmarks of judicial misogyny: "They did not defile the girl. She was a mere cistern for foul toads to knot and gender in" (*State v. Snow*, 1923, p. 632). Even with children, the courts have been cruel with regard to rape.

Consent

Legal preoccupation with the character of the victim is a significant factor in the issue of consent. If a woman consents to sexual activity in any way, then she cannot claim to be raped. The male fear of the vindictive or spurned lover or the female temptress who gives all the implicit cues to consent yet later claims rape, gives rise to a variety of standards that require the victim's testimony be confirmed by other evidence to convict. Modern statutes may not require corroborative evidence of resistance, but often some indication must be given of nonconsent. Evidence of resistance is regarded as evidence of nonconsent. Torn clothing, bruises, red marks, vaginal tears, or blood stains (indicating lack of lubrication) can provide evidence of nonconsent. These indicators support her assertion that she did not consent, even though the perpetrator says she did, and make it easier for the judge and jury to believe her. Several scholars have pointed out the difficulty of interpreting even this physical evidence in light of the fact that sex is a contact activity. This quality of sexual contact complicates the idea of resistance and force. Estrich (1987) notes that physical contact, if not force, is implied in the sexual act: "Certainly, if a thief stripped his victim, flattened that victim on the floor, lay down on top, and took the victim's wallet or jewelry, few would pause before concluding forcible robbery"

(p. 59). Estrich also emphasizes that the issue of consent involves a male using force against a female. These are usually persons of different stature, physical strength, and perhaps even self-confidence, who might have very different visions of what is adequate or appropriate "resistance" under the circumstances.

Bohmer (1991) provides an interesting hypothetical example regarding how problematic the issue of "force" is:

> If one is told that a person had intercourse with someone who tied her down, that information would not be enough to determine whether the intercourse was forced. One first needs to know the details of the circumstances whereby the woman was tied down. Or did she attempt to resist the force used to tie her down against her will? Even asking the participants themselves will not necessarily provide the answer. The woman might say that she did not want to be tied down and the man might say that she did. What she intended as resistance he interpreted as part of the game he thought they were playing to heighten their sexual pleasure. Both interpretations are plausible. (pp. 319-320)

Even Alex Comfort's (1972) best-selling book, *The Joy of Sex*, is replete with examples of bondage and "rape games."

Thus, numerous problems are encountered when using force and resistance as a standard. Both sex and rape are activities in which force is inherent and, in some cases, may be extreme and in which the parties have unequal physical power in the activity.

The other aspect of consent are the myths regarding how women approach sexual relations. Consent and the preliminary refusals are often given nonverbally; direct discussion is often considered tactless and embarrassing. This convention may fuel part of the "enchantress" myth of rape victims—namely, that they asked for it. Despite the sexual revolution, it is surprising the degree to which the "madonna/whore" archetypes prevail.

Arguing consent as a defense in the New Bedford, Massachusetts, rape case in which a woman was gang raped on a pool table in a bar among the cheers of patrons, indicates the level to which a "she's asking for it" myth can extend. A further example can be seen in a recent law review article:

On October 4, 1989, a jury in Fort Lauderdale, Florida, acquitted a
Georgia man of charges he kidnapped and sexually assaulted a
Broward County woman at knife point. The acquittal itself might
have had limited affect had it not been for the statement made by
the jury foreman after the verdict was announced: "She asked for it,"
he claimed; "she was advertising for sex." Another juror agreed; "We
felt she was up to no good (by) the way she was dressed." (Fromm,
1991, p. 579)

Thus, a woman's behavior determines her character, which in
turn determines her likelihood of implicitly consenting to sex. In
these situations, men are generally considered helplessly controlled
by their sexual impulses and therefore by the "temptress" allure. To
use a prior example, it would not occur to a jury that if someone
wearing a diamond stickpin were walking down the street, the
robber of that stickpin would be absolved of the crime. Yet, this
attitude often persists in some rape case decisions. The natural
consequence of this logic is that beaches where women are dressed
scantily would become open hunting grounds for predatory rapists.
To find out "what kind of woman this victim is" and whether she is
the type to have consented to sex under these circumstances, the
courts have in the past allowed defense attorneys free rein in explor-
ing the sexual life of the victim.

Rape Shield Laws

All states now have some form of rape shield laws. These laws
resulted from the humiliating tactics of some defense counsels by
introducing evidence of the victim's sexual history to blemish her
character, to reduce jury sympathy, and to imply that she was the
kind of woman who would have consented to sex with the perpetrator ("The Rape Shield Paradox," 1987). Rape shield laws represent legislation that has a special provision for limiting the admissibility of evidence concerning the victim's sexual conduct with
persons other than the defendant. The evidence of past consensual
sex with others is not deemed relevant to whether she consented
with this perpetrator unless there was a pattern of this behavior on

her part. Most states make similar exceptions, typically after a special meeting or hearing on the unique relevance of this evidence by the defense. This meeting or hearing, known as *in camera* sessions, will take place before the judge but not the jury.

Rape shield laws in various states have been effective in keeping out of the public trial evidence concerning a woman's general sexual reputation in the community, specific acts of prior sex with men other than the defendant, as well as prior acts of prostitution (*State v. Romer,* 1980) and prior convictions for prostitution (*Johnson v. State,* 1979). Some courts have allowed evidence of sexual contact with others shortly before the time period in which the rape occurred to show a motive for bias (*Commonwealth v. Taylor,* 1985) or a pattern of behavior (*People v. Varon,* 1983). In general practice, however, if the defense goes through the trouble of requesting a pretrial hearing on evidence that is likely to enter the trial, the courts' bias is to admit any evidence that has at least some relevance. Many rape shield laws have an exception that allows the court to balance the privacy rights of the victim with the defendant's right to a fair trial. The statutes may in fact only be keeping out the most flagrant harassment. An indirect impact of the shield laws is to increase the number of pleas bargained and therefore lower sentences. This allows the victim to avoid the ordeal of a trial and the defendant, if incarcerated, to receive a lighter sentence (Feild & Bienen, 1980).

Unique Problems
of Acquaintance Rape

Estrich (1987) notes that "real rape" occurs when a stranger leaps from the bushes with a knife, not when a date goes bad. Courts have a difficult time with rapes that occur between people who would be acceptable sexual partners. By virtue of the relationship of the perpetrator and victim, the burden of proof appears to shift toward the victim.

Part of this shift is due to prevalent cultural attitudes about rape. The acquaintance rape myth discussed in an earlier chapter that "No" means "Yes," is part of a belief that women will not admit to consent, given societal attitudes toward women who consent too freely. Consequently,

> what she may see as a refusal, he may see as socially appropriate coyness. In such a situation he may go ahead and press her further. The outcome, sexual intercourse, which she considers forced, may be viewed by him—and participants in the courtroom who share his cultural attitudes—as consensual sex. (Bohmer, 1991, pp. 321-322)

This shift in burden takes place by not focusing on the perpetrator's intent but rather placing the burden on the prosecutor to show that the victim did not consent. Current law does not appear to recognize that "being sexually penetrated without consent is a grave harm; and that being treated like an object whose words are not even worthy of consideration adds insult to injury" (Estrich, 1987, p. 98). Forced sex by an acquaintance is not seen as the same as forced sex by a stranger.

Where there has been prior sexual activity between the participants, the intimate details of the encounters will be allowed under virtually all rape shield laws. Hence, acquaintance rape occurring in the context of a date ensures that there will be some detailed examination of the victim's sexual conduct at least with regard to the defendant. The basis of this rule is that if a woman consented to sex with a man once, she is likely to have consented during the time in question. The implication is that once a woman consents to sex with a man, she loses, or has greatly diminished, legal protection from future sexual penetration by this man. California law represents one exception to this trend. This legislation states that a current or previous dating relationship is not sufficient as consent in and of itself in the matter of rape (*California Penal Code*, 1991).

In some states, including California, the defense of mistake or reasonable belief in consent can be raised. Reasonable belief is an affirmative defense that the defendant raises. If the defendant can show that he had a reasonable and good-faith belief the woman voluntarily consented to engage in sex, then he did not have the prerequisite intent to commit the crime of rape.

Marital Rape

Included in the problem of acquaintance rape is rape in the most intimate of all relationships—marriage. As previously noted, according to common law, a man could not rape his wife. States have been successful to varying degrees in removing the marital exclusion for rape from their laws. This change in legislation has been difficult to enact because husbands have had an immunity from having their wives testify against them. In addition, some states have held that marriage is a contract providing for, among other things, sexual services and that any law changing that contract violates the Constitution (Burt, 1985).

The degree of protection provided by marital rape laws varies considerably from state to state. At one end of the spectrum, some states require parties to either be divorced or legally separated before such charges can be brought, whereas other states will allow spouses to make charges while cohabiting and married.

Marital rape cases pose several problems. Rape shield laws do not apply because the parties have a sexual history together. Extramarital affairs may be used to indicate bias or motive for charging rape (Burt, 1985). Furthermore, if the wife is in the process of securing a divorce, the defense may well use this fact stating that the rape charge is being brought by the wife to secure a better position in the divorce proceedings.

Victims of marital rape are abused by the publicity surrounding these cases. Of the 4,500 letters received by the Rideouts—parties in the first marital rape case—80% treated the matter as a joke (Burt, 1985). Despite all these obstacles, 88% of the marital rape cases studied by the National Clearinghouse on Marital and Date Rape between 1978 and 1985 ended in conviction. The high percentage of these convictions, higher even than other types of rape cases, may in part be due to the ferocity of the domestic violence that was a component in these rapes and the tendency of the police only to arrest in the most extreme marital rape cases (Russell, 1991). Although rape can legally occur in marriage without actual violence, similar to acquaintance rape, marital rape is only treated seriously when brutal violence occurs.

The Legal Processing
of Acquaintance Rape Cases

Acquaintance rape is perhaps the most underreported major crime. *Ms. Magazine's* "Campus Report on Sexual Assault," using a sample of 7,000 college-age women, reported that one in eight had been raped according to the legal definition of the term and more than 90% did not report their assault to the police (Koss, Gidycz, & Wisniewski, 1987). Acquaintance rape victims deciding to pursue criminal rape charges must follow several steps.

The first step is reporting the crime to the police. The police have the discretion, based on their investigation, of determining whether the charge is founded or unfounded. If the investigation reveals the charge is founded, the case will be passed on to the prosecutor.

The investigation of the charge by the police presents unique problems for the victim. One study of a major metropolitan police force revealed the investigation of a rape case is affected by three factors: the promptness of the complaint, the physical condition and medical evidence of the complaint, and the prior behavior of the victim ("Police Discretion," 1968). Following the report of a rape to the police, an officer will typically be dispatched. The amount of delay that has lapsed between the crime and when the complaint is reported, however, will determine the rapidity with which the police can respond. Although many victims prefer to work with a female police officer, in some areas the delay in securing a female officer might prejudice the victim's case and may not be warranted (Lopez, 1992). Although evidence of the rape trauma syndrome may not be introduced at trial to prove the victim was raped, it may sometimes be introduced to contradict the traditional belief of how a woman should have reacted when raped. Rape trauma syndrome describes a particular type of posttraumatic stress disorder experienced by victims of sexual assault. Initially, the victim may go into denial after the rape and be simply unable to believe the attack has occurred (McLaughlin, 1991). The victim may then experience intense feelings of disgust, embarrassment, and humiliation that affect her ability to report the crime immediately (Burgess & Holmstrom, 1974). As indicated earlier, if the victim was intoxicated, this can be a significant factor in the investigation of rape reports. Of complaints being judged unfounded, 82% involved situations where the victim was reported to have been intoxicated at the time of the rape ("Police Discretion," 1968).

Following the rape report, the victim will usually be taken by police to a hospital for a medical and evidentiary examination. Many communities have hospitals that have established sexual assault units with medical personnel skilled in sensitively dealing with rape victims and the use of a "rape kit" for evidentiary examination and preservation. If the victim's clothes have not been washed, semen and blood may still be available for evidence. In some hospitals, a rape advocate affiliated with the local rape crisis center will meet the woman before she undergoes the examination. A rape advocate can provide important emotional support to the victim as she deals with the trauma of her assault and begins the legal process of prosecuting her assailant (Lopez, 1992).

Following the medical examination, a detective generally attached to the police department's sex crimes unit will complete the investigation and will turn the case over to the prosecutor's office who must determine whether to prosecute the crime (Lopez, 1992). The prosecutor must determine if there is sufficient evidence to convince a jury that a rape occurred beyond a reasonable doubt. Factors such as uncorroborated testimony, the absence of physical evidence showing resistance or vaginal tears due to the lack of lubrication, evidence of drug or alcohol use, or a prior relationship between the victim and perpetrator make convictions difficult to achieve. In 1985, only 38% of all men arrested for rape nationwide were prosecuted for a felony (Taylor, 1987). If the prosecutor sees a prosecutable case, the next step is submitting the case to the judge and jury.

If there is a reasonable suspicion that a crime has been committed, the police will seek the arrest of the perpetrator. An arrest warrant will be issued on the basis of a grand jury indictment or a document, called an "information," will be filed with the court by the prosecutor. The accused will be taken into custody and booked. Booking implies that a record is made of the arrest and identifying information, including fingerprints, and pictures are taken. Usually within a short time after arrest, the accused is taken before a magistrate and arraigned. Arraignment consists of the accused being told what the charges are against him, asking how he pleads, whether and what bail will be set, and informing him that an attorney will be assigned him, if he cannot afford his own.

If arrested on the basis of an "information," the court will then hold a preliminary hearing to determine if there is a case for trial. The rape victim may be called to this hearing to present testimony and to help the judge determine if a crime has been committed. Given that the judge finds reasonable cause for binding the suspect over for trial, it is likely a jury will be impaneled.

A jury brings to the criminal justice system its collective wisdom as well as all of the diverse prejudices and biases of the community at large. For example, research shows that where the victim was seen as being friendly to the rapist prior to the rape, jurors' verdicts were lenient toward the rapists, regardless of the strength of the evidence of forcible rape (Feild & Bienen, 1980). To the jury, the victim's prior sexual conduct with the defendant or others, if it is allowed to be introduced, can have the most destructive effect. The use of evidence regarding the victim's character distracts the jury from the issue of consent during the alleged rape (Wiener, 1983). One researcher concluded in her examination of date rape prosecutions that the major defense strategy remains one of "trying the victim" (Lopez, 1992, p. 301). This circumstance complicates the cost-benefit analysis that victims must go through in deciding to prosecute their assailant.

In the event the defendant is convicted, in some states the victim can request the opportunity to present her pleas for punishment (or leniency) to the court. Typically, this would be done through the prosecuting attorney (for punishment) or the defense attorney (for leniency). Victims pleading for leniency would probably be more likely in circumstances where the defendant confessed to police or pled guilty at the trial. This is also more likely to occur where the prosecution has not consulted with the victim in any way. The court's agreement to accept this testimony can be problematic in acquaintance rape cases because such pleas may be motivated by coercion or ostracism from mutual acquaintances expressing their bias about the rape as a victim-precipitated crime.

Pros and Cons of
Reporting Acquaintance Rape

Acquaintance rape victims are faced with a difficult choice when deciding whether or not to report their assault. The primary benefit of reporting involves empowering the victim to regain control over her life by affirmatively pursuing a course of action that punishes the perpetrator for his offense. A successful conviction might lead to incarceration of the rapist and will send a message to the rapist and others that the court will punish acquaintance rapists for wrongdoing. In some cases, a conviction or plea bargain may lead to the rapist being forced into treatment, thereby hopefully diminishing his propensity to rape again. Even if the conviction fails or the police believe the complaint is unfounded, repeated reports on a defendant by different women will require the police to take notice and more fully investigate the matter.

Once the criminal proceeding begins, the victim simply becomes the prosecution's main witness, and the victim transfers control over the case to the state. Although frustrating at times, this also means that the victim does not need to assume responsibility for the process to proceed and can deny having control to friends and family members.

The costs incurred from reporting are that it is likely the complaint will not be filed and that the victim may experience disbelief on the part of officials and her social network. In addition, rape shield laws may be circumvented in certain circumstances that may lead to the victim being tried at a high emotional price to her. The victim must also be prepared for possible negative reactions from her social network—especially when the perpetrator and victim share friends and acquaintances.

Once the legal process is started, the victim will find it difficult to maintain any control over the case. This can be very frustrating and any sympathy shown by the victim toward the rapist may jeopardize the conviction. As already discussed, acquaintance rape has a low conviction rate and high visibility. Finally, failure to get a conviction or have the complaint identified as unfounded, may be used against the woman in the future, should she be raped again, to show she falsely cries rape in such situations.

The pros and cons of whether or not to prosecute the perpetrator must be considered relatively quickly by the victim because delay in reporting indicates to some juries and police officers that rape in fact may not have occurred, thereby reducing the effectiveness of that option in states that do not allow rape trauma syndrome testimony. Such testimony can be used to explain the reasonableness or expectability of the delayed reporting of victims.

Rape as Personal Wrong

Rape is not only a crime, but a personal injury against the victim. Sexual assault constitutes a battery—an intentional harmful or offensive contact with the woman's body. In addition to processing the case through criminal court, a victim may use the civil court system to obtain financial damages for injury resulting from the rape. Damages may include emotional distress and medical expenses for treatment as well as lost wages from work and, in some cases, punitive damages, defined as damages to punish the offender. Punitive damages can result in sizable financial awards. In at least one case, a woman sued several attackers and the renter in whose apartment the attack had taken place and who made no attempt to stop the attack. The plaintiff obtained a jury verdict of $300,000 (Loggans, 1985).

Rape shield laws do not apply to civil cases. Therefore, the victim's sexual history with the defendant and others is likely to become an issue. However, the burden of proof in a civil case is lower. A preponderance of the evidence is required in civil cases compared to proof beyond a reasonable doubt in criminal cases. Theoretically at least, a case that would not meet the level of a criminal conviction could still meet the level of a civil judgment of liability.

In certain situations, for example, fraternity gang rapes, third parties such as the university or fraternity may be sued. Such lawsuits can be helpful to the victim because if the jury provides a large verdict, the university is likely to be able to pay for it. However, because there are so few cases of this nature, it is difficult to get such a conviction and to predict the legal consequences of such an action.

Cases where there might have been a verdict against the third party are likely to have been settled out of court. Universities are unlikely to expose themselves to such bad publicity. When deciding the amount of damages, the court may well allow expert testimony of the rape trauma syndrome to indicate the level of damages appropriate, given the prospects of long-term injury. Depending on the coping ability of the victim and the level of support she receives from her environment, the posttraumatic fear and anxiety following a rape, part of the rape trauma syndrome, can last many years (McLaughlin, 1991).

Acquaintance Rape and Civil Court

A civil case generally goes through the following stages: complaint, service, answer, discovery, pretrial settlement conference, and a trial on liability and damages. There are also likely to be motions regarding the admissibility and relevance of evidence.

When filing a case in civil court, a victim must hire a private attorney and tell the attorney her story. The attorney will draft a document setting out the reasons for the lawsuit and the damages requested. This document is filed with the court and then is generally served by a sheriff's deputy on the accused, now called the defendant. The defendant must then file and serve (often on the woman's attorney through registered mail) his own document, an answer, which sets out his defenses to the accusations. The lawsuit is now begun in earnest and a time is set aside for discovery of the evidence each has against the other.

The discovery may take several forms and include interrogatories (written questions that are answered in writing under oath and returned); depositions (where a party or witness is interrogated by the attorneys under oath and questions and answers are recorded by a court recorder); subpoenas of documents, or both or, in some cases, medical or psychiatric examinations of either or both parties.

Following these procedures, a trial date is set by the victim's attorney. Before the trial takes place, attorneys often hold special hearings before the judge to determine the admissibility of certain types of evidence. A pretrial conference is typically held just prior to the trial (which may be before a judge alone or a jury) for the purpose of determining if a settlement can be reached between the parties without a trial. The trier of fact (judge alone or jury) will determine if a defendant is liable for the injury, and if so for how much of the injury. For example, in the case *Morris v. Yogi Bear's Jellystone Park* (Pfeiffer, 1990), a 13-year-old female was awarded damages for being raped by three 17-year-old males but was found to be 12% at fault herself. Once liability is determined, the trier of fact determines the amount of damages.

Pros and Cons of Pursuing
Civil Action in Acquaintance Rape

When pursuing legal actions in acquaintance rape cases, it is likely that the victim will need to file criminal rape charges so as not to prejudice her case in civil court. Hence, the logic of what she would be expected to do if she really did not consent must be confronted. As there is no rape shield law in civil cases, the victim may be confronted with the humiliation of describing her sex life on the stand, should the court feel this is relevant to whether she consented or to the level of damages requested. The victim will still have to prove a rape occurred. She will need to hire a private attorney. Unless the attorney feels that there is a substantial probability of receiving a large damage award against a defendant who in fact can pay the award, the attorney is unlikely to take a contingent fee contract, unless the attorney is committed to this type of work. A contingent fee agreement means that the client will only pay for court and expert fees but will forfeit one third to one half of the final award to the attorney as fees. Otherwise, the victim will have to pay for representation on an hourly basis. Persons working with acquaintance rape victims should have some knowledge of attorneys who would be willing to pursue such actions for altruistic reasons.

As already discussed, the benefits of initiating a civil law suit against the rapist include the following: The victim faces a lower standard of proof, damages will be paid directly to the victim that may enable her to get on with her life, and the victim remains in control of the case throughout the process. Because the rapist cannot be incarcerated, there might be less disruption of the woman's social network by going the civil court route.

Mediation of
Acquaintance Rape Cases

A possible alternative to criminal court action in acquaintance rape cases is mediation. Because acquaintance rape often involves people who will be in contact with each other in the future or who at least will have social networks in common, mediation may be one mechanism for resolving the conflict. Mediation involves the use of a neutral third party to assist the victim and perpetrator to reach an agreement that is in both of their interests. Rape is not typically mediated in criminal proceedings as such. Rather, these cases generally are mediated as simple assault cases without rape ever being directly addressed. Mediated settlement of a civil action is most likely to take place. Because to get to this stage of resolution a criminal rape charge has been made and a civil battery complaint filed and served, mediation occurs at the end of a long process.

Mediation may serve several purposes. The perpetrator may wish to use mediation as a way to avoid a civil rape trial. For the victim, mediation can avoid the embarrassment of a public trial with an uncertain outcome. Other favorable outcomes to the use of mediation include a monetary award for restitution and the payment of attorney fees, a confession of guilt from the perpetrator that may assist the victim in her recovery process, reimbursement to the victim for professional fees related to her recovery, and the issuance of a restraining order providing the victim protection in the future.

The mediation of an acquaintance rape case can be very delicate in that small errors can cause large problems. An acquaintance rape represents the perpetrator exercising control and force over the victim, placing the latter in a humiliating position. In mediation, this power differential between the perpetrator and victim can become an issue because both parties must be equally involved in the negotiating that forms the basis of mediation (Milne, Salem, & Koeffler, 1992). Considering the power differential that exists, in mediation the victim exposes herself to further victimization from coercion, or even insult from the perpetrator. The victim must be aware that mediation will involve her confronting the perpetrator. This can be physically and emotionally very stressful. The presence of a rape counselor may be helpful to the victim in this process.

Despite these costs, there are numerous benefits of mediation in acquaintance rape situations, including the following: (a) the perpetrator could potentially absolve the victim of her role in the rape; (b) a settlement may be negotiated that might be difficult for a court to do; and (c) mediation allows the parties concerned to directly control the outcome of the proceeding and, in some cases, allows the victim to express rage and anger at the offender so that he can experience the enormity of his action.

A problem in mediation, however, is the difficulty in finding someone willing to conduct the mediation and the possible fallout from the court system. The hesitancy in presenting mediation as an alternative in acquaintance rape cases comes from the possibility that if such a procedure was helpful in a few selected cases, then the court system could begin ordering mediation as mandatory. If mediation of acquaintance rape cases became mandatory, the seriousness of the lawsuit might be diminished and the abuses or costs previously discussed may likely occur. In addition, mediation opens up the possibility that criminal charges in acquaintance rape cases would be diminished in severity with the result that such cases would regularly be referred to mediation. It is with this caution, that mediation is suggested as a possible alternative to a civil trial.

Summary

This chapter has presented the different legal options available to acquaintance rape victims and the difficult decision-making process that confronts them. Human service professionals working with acquaintance rape victims should be aware of the legal process specific to the state and locale in which the victim resides.

Historically, the role of a rape victim in the judicial system has been a very difficult one. Currently, that role, and the obstacles that acquaintance rape victims face, has been reduced by legal reform.

However, the path is still a painful one. Sensitive support from counselors, victim advocates, and other professionals can help acquaintance rape victims as they pursue prosecution of their assailant. The law still remains leery of rape victims who have been traditionally seen as precipitating the rape and will continue to place a high burden on victims for some time to come. However, it is always important to have supportive help to identify the legal tactics as just that—legal tactics—and to not see such strategies as confirmation of the victim's guilt or the rapist's innocence. Only through a pattern of successfully making acquaintance rape a punishable crime with compensable personal injury, can the law support a change in attitude regarding women's ability to control sexual access to their own bodies.

Note

1. Although there are constitutional reasons why rape statutes must treat the rape victim and rapist as androgynous, for the purposes of this discussion, the victim will be a female and the perpetrator a male. Historically this has been so, and feminist scholars have provided very useful analyses of the inequity of treatment of victims on the basis of this distinction.

Seeking counseling after being raped is the best gift you can give yourself.
—An acquaintance rape survivor

9 The Counselor in the Recovery Process

The Counselor/Client Relationship

The counselor-to-client connection is like no other intimate relationship. It is neither parent to child, friend to friend, nor teacher to pupil, although counseling may, at times, reflect elements of all of these relationships. The counselor/client alliance is unique, and it is important to conceptualize the relationship in a way that reflects our professional values and beliefs and informs our judgments about effective interventions. The acquaintance rape survivor who seeks counseling is especially vulnerable to the power issues that are inherent in any helping relationship. For this reason it is essential that a collaborative relationship be established between counselor and survivor with an intervention model that empowers the survivor and sees her as an active participant in her own healing (Ellis & "Eve," 1990; Laidlaw, Malmo, & Associates, 1990). The counselor's role then is to provide guidance and support, with a commitment to the belief that the client knows what hurts and what helps, that she has all that she needs within herself for healing, and that what she needs most from the counselor is the safety to openly express herself and to experience the validation of her worth and value (Laidlaw et al., 1990).

In keeping with the foregoing concept of the counselor/client relationship as a healing partnership, this book promotes an approach to intervention that has been described as *feminist therapy* (Laidlaw et al., 1990). Although the term is gender-specific, we believe that this approach applies to more than women counselors working with women clients. In our view, the term feminist therapy describes a model for psychosocial intervention that most effectively empowers both the client and the counselor to effectively define and pace the recovery process, creates a participatory and equal relationship between the counselor and client of mutual trust and respect, and provides a safe environment for the disclosure of deeply personal experiences and the expression of painful feelings.[1] It might also be described as *humanist therapy,* although that would not adequately acknowledge its roots in feminist literature and could be confused with other theoretical orientations.

Feminist therapy is distinguished by its underlying assumptions about the source of most problems that people bring to mental health practitioners. These assumptions challenge more traditional therapies that typically fail to acknowledge that much of the personal dysfunctioning presented by mental health clients is the result of societal and family dysfunctioning. The *destructive circumstances* created by power imbalances in homes, schools, churches, places of work, and in society in general, are manifested in clients' self-defeating attempts to cope and survive. Maladaptive coping and surviving efforts then emerge as mental health problems or problems-in-living (Laidlaw et al., 1990).

A feminist approach to interventions with women assumes that many of the mental health problems presented by women are primarily problems of self-identity and individuation. The depression and anxiety seen in women are believed to be typically due to a socialization process that teaches women that they are powerless to affect the circumstances of their lives and that they must expect to defer to the needs of others. The education of women to accommodate the emotional and sexual needs of men results in a loss of respect for one's own needs and feelings and a lifelong seeking for approval and acceptance from males. The emotional dependency of women on men for validation and self-worth frequently results in destructive and abusive relationships that undermine a woman's mental and emotional health. In the case of acquaintance rape, a woman brings to the recovery process all of her past learning and experience about male/female relationships that influence her response to the rape and that affect her resources for effective recovery.

In the feminist or participatory approach to interventions, the relationship between counselor and client is one of equality and mutuality. Although the counselor assumes primary responsibility for guiding the recovery process because of her specialized knowledge and skills, she does so in a way that bridges the professional distance between herself and the client. She avoids a position of power that diminishes the client as a person and as the primary actor in her own recovery (Laidlaw et al., 1990). It is important to recognize, however, that persons who have a long history of relationships that were extremely imbalanced may be limited in their ability to make use of an equal power relationship, because they have no basis for trusting others to respect and value them. Such persons may appear resistant or unresponsive to intervention. The skillful counselor who can communicate trustworthiness and respect in the early stages of recovery can usually correct negative and distorted perceptions of interpersonal relationships that some persons bring to their recovery work.

The counselor who is prepared to establish a healing partnership with a survivor of acquaintance rape and who can develop an atmosphere of safety with mutual trust and respect is one with deep convictions about the effective use of self. She sees herself as an instrument of healing (Cournoyer, 1989), and she realizes that she, like the client, brings to each and every psychosocial intervention and each and every client the sum total of her own learning and experience that will either facilitate or hinder the recovery process. The effectiveness of intervention will depend on the dynamics of the counseling relationship characterized by genuine caring and empathy, mutual positive regard and respect, shared decision making, and fresh and creative approaches to intervention (Corey, Corey, & Callanan, 1984).

The remainder of this chapter will focus on specific concerns that relate to the counselor's knowledge, skills, values, and attitudes. These concerns assume that the counselor is prepared to honestly consider certain important questions if there is to be an effective and mutually empowering use of self in the recovery process. Although we are using the feminine pronouns to refer to the counselor, all of the material in this chapter is transferable to male counselors.

Concerns for the Counselor

Because of the special circumstances that typically surround each incident of acquaintance rape, the counselor should be prepared to respond to each survivor with a thorough understanding of the dynamics of acquaintance rape but without preconceived assumptions about what may be true for *this* survivor in *this* situation. The counselor's response should, therefore, be person-specific and free from any formulaic approach, with an appreciation for the individual nature of each victimizing experience. There is wide variation in how persons respond to trauma, depending on both personal and environmental factors. A knowledge of the victim's unique personal history, her personality, her situation, and her special needs will significantly influence the helping process. This is not to deny, however, the *pattern* of response to rape. Understanding the typical experiences that victims share at each stage of healing helps to normalize what the survivor is thinking and feeling and helps her to be aware of what may lie ahead with such tentative statements as, "You may feel . . ." or "Many survivors find that they . . ." Such awareness provides a measure of self-control and self-mastery and facilitates recovery from what is typically inevitable and predictable in the healing process.

The counselor must appreciate the complex dynamics of acquaintance rape. Unlike stranger rape, when responsibility for the victimization is clearly the perpetrators', the dynamics of acquaintance rape are typically ambiguous and often confusing. This is because of the familiar and often intimate relationship between victim and perpetrator that makes it difficult for the victim herself, as well as others, to define the sexual activity as rape and makes it likely that the victim will blame herself or be blamed by others for her victimization. Also, in contrast to stranger rape, and because of the familiar relationships between victim and perpetrator, the woman is more personally involved in the sexual encounter. This means that she is more likely to be seen as responsible for the incident (Calhoun & Townsley, 1991).

The appropriate attribution of responsibility for the rape to the perpetrator rather than to the victim typically depends on other people in the victim's life who can respond to her needs with understanding and sensitivity. Such a person is often in a counseling/ advocacy role with the victim. The success of the recovery process is based on a positive interpersonal dynamic between counselor and victim that requires acknowledging the reality of the rape and knowing what to do to help the survivor recover. For the counselor, this primary concern is the reservoir of all her knowledge, as well as the skills and values, that she brings to her work and to the acquaintance rape victim who is seeking her help. This concern will include the following issues:

1. Do I have sufficient knowledge and skills to respond effectively to acquaintance rape victims? What are the limits of my position and (in certain cases) my gender?

Knowledge and Skills. Essential knowledge for the counselor includes an understanding of the rape trauma syndrome and the symptoms manifested in the acute, reorganizing, and integration phases; the effects of previous sexual assault(s) that complicate recovery and predispose the survivor to revictimization; the dynamics of acquaintance rape that are typically demonstrated in victim blaming; and the response from family, friends, and community that can either enhance or interfere with the recovery process. Important skills for working with acquaintance rape victims include the ability to accurately assess such factors as the victim's prior history and functioning, the meaning of the rape for her sense of self and her relationships with others, the condition of her circumstances and life-functioning needs, and her ability to use recovery strategies and resources. In addition to assessment skills, the effective counselor will be prepared to educate the client, to provide "positive mirroring," and to have a repertoire of interventions that effectively assist the victim in her approach/avoidance process of resolution and integration (Janoff-Bulman, 1992).

The Agency. The limits to intervention are frequently determined by the nature of the counselor's agency, by the counselor's gender, and by the counselor's training and expertise. It is essential that anyone in the position of a helper be prepared to provide crisis intervention, to link a victim to crisis services or both. Rape counseling, long-term intervention, or both are most effectively provided by persons with specialized training whenever such services are available.

Gender Issues. Factors related to gender may also affect the counseling process. If the counselor is the same sex as the perpetrator, the client may transfer feelings of anger, fear, and mistrust to the counselor. This is especially likely early in the recovery process. However, the counselor who is the same gender as the perpetrator may, in some instances, provide an important corrective emotional experience by being trustworthy, respectful, and empathic. The counselor in these situation may have to work hard to develop a healing relationship, but there may be an important payoff when the client is helped in a special way.

In all cases in which gender can be an issue, the following apply:

- The survivor should, if possible, have a choice of gender if both male and female counselors are available.
- When gender factors could affect the counseling relationship, the counselor should be prepared to maintain good boundaries. This includes being aware of and dealing with issues of transference, including the possibility of a romantic or parent/child attachment.
- If a referral to another counselor is advisable and available, the counselor should in all cases act in the client's best interest. (Dolan, 1992)

Gender issues are often a factor when clergy are called on to counsel sexual assault survivors, because both clergy and perpetrators are most often males. However, clergy are often the first persons sexual assault victims turn to for help. Because a clergyperson is a trusted and familiar resource, parishioners assume he or she will know what to do in times of crisis. Many times, especially in small towns and rural areas, clergy are the only helpers available, although they may be inadequately prepared to respond to a victim or perpetrator of acquaintance rape.[2] In their efforts to hasten resolution and to offer a religious solution, clergy will often prescribe premature forgiveness before the victim is ready and without the perpetrator's acknowledgment of responsibility. This can leave the victim feeling betrayed and confused and offers the perpetrator absolution without accountability. The clergy's lack of expertise in responding to the crisis of sexual assault is related to a lack of specialized professional training that is typical of seminaries and ministerial training programs. Such educational programs usually offer training in counseling but typically lack content in rape crisis intervention. Some degree of specialized knowledge about rape trauma and recovery is necessary to respond sensitively and to provide basic information and assistance. Many helping professionals, clergy included, are not aware that sexual violence trauma is like no other trauma (Fortune, 1983). Unfortunately, this lack of specialized training about sexual violence is true for most of the helping professions. Public awareness and educational programs sponsored by rape crisis centers help to close this knowledge gap, and professional staff are usually available for training programs.

It is also true, however, that rape crisis counselors frequently find that they must respond to needs that are beyond their training and expertise. Survivors, for example, who have histories of past sexual victimization or other kinds of past abuse, are often in need of intense, long-term psychological intervention that may be beyond the capacity of the rape crisis center and its staff. In such cases, rape counselors must be prepared to network with community mental health agencies, with private therapists, or both for consultation and referral. A more complete discussion of the various levels and modalities of intervention will be provided in the next chapter.

    2. What are my attitudes and beliefs about sexual victimization and how have they been influenced by my personal experiences?

Self-Awareness. Self-awareness is an essential personal attribute for any helping professional. The counselor in any setting who is out of touch with her own needs and feelings about human sexuality and sexual victimization is likely to be at best ineffective and at worst harmful in her response to acquaintance rape victims. It is not unusual for the counselor to bring to her work a history of sexual abuse. (This is true as well for male counselors.) To the extent that the helper has taken her own healing journey, she will be able to travel that journey with another survivor with compassion and confidence. However, the counselor who has been sexually victimized must be aware of the risks her own victimization may present to the client's recovery, including the tendency to self-disclose indiscriminately, and to confuse her own experience with the client's. When this occurs, the client's recovery is overlaid with the counselor's own unfinished business.

Self-disclosure by the counselor is always risky and is best used infrequently, if at all, and only when it is in the best interest of the client to do so. Once the counselor discloses her own past trauma, a shift in focus can easily occur from the client's needs to the counselor's. When this happens, the client begins caring for the counselor. Such a situation may replicate other boundary violations that the survivor has experienced, including the rape itself. Also, the client may compare her own experiences of trauma and recovery with that of the counselor and feel either angry or inadequate (Dolan, 1992).

The counselor, in any setting, who has unresolved issues with her own victimization must be willing to recognize her vulnerabilities and determine if she needs to seek the help of another counselor for her own recovery. The counselor's unfinished business may include lingering tendencies to deny or diminish her own victimization or a persistent need to self-blame and to suppress feelings of shame or anger. To not accept responsibility for one's own recovery is to risk either overreacting and becoming overinvolved in the victim's situation or denying, diminishing, and distancing from the victim's experience.

Many helping professionals have been victims of some form of abuse. The help professionals receive for painful experiences can in

turn help them understand and empathize with clients more effectively. Counselors' past abusive experiences can be a hindrance to
effective helping because these experiences may predispose them to
overidentification and loss of boundaries in their work with clients.
The helping relationship involves a conscious and deliberate use of
the self. For counselors to use themselves effectively and reduce the
risk of harm to clients and themselves, they must have a very good
understanding of themselves and a well-developed capacity for
interpersonal self-discipline. Although most people can neglect such
self-understanding and self-discipline, this is not possible for individuals working in the helping professions. The effectiveness of the
counselor's work and the well-being of the counselor depends on it
(Cournoyer, 1989).

The helping professional in any field—psychiatry, psychology, social work, law, medicine, nursing, theology, education—who has unresolved issues and myth-laden attitudes toward male/female relationships and sexual victimization, risks responding to victims with
denial of their victimization, subtle or not so subtle blame, or both.

Helpers should consider the following questions as a guide for
examining their attitudes and the way they may affect the client:

- To what extent do I identify with the victim or with the offender?
- What personal experiences have I had that enable me to relate to the
  victim's feelings of being powerless, fearful, and alone?
- What beliefs about sexual violence have I accepted that may be based
  on myth rather than fact, for example, the belief that women ask to be
  raped by the way they behave or the clothes they wear or the belief
  that rapists can't control their sexual urges?

The counselor must respond to victims of sexual assault in a calm
and knowledgeable way and without feelings of anger, disgust, or
discomfort. It is important for the victim to believe that the person
to whom she has turned for help believes her, will support her in a
nonjudgmental way, and knows what to do (Fortune, 1983).

3. Am I willing to work with acquaintance rape survivors, to believe
   their stories, and to empathize with their pain?

Many counselors find themselves working with victims of sexual assault without consciously deciding to do so. The reality is that sexual assault victims may well seek help at some time for problems associated with their sexual victimization. A deep conviction that healing is possible and a vision that sees their clients whole and strong are important attitudes for counselors in their work with acquaintance rape survivors. Counselors must be prepared to hear and believe stories from survivors that may be filled with horror and with cruel and twisted details of victimization, stories that the ordinary person tends to disbelieve and discount as exaggeration and perhaps even fantasy. Counselors must be willing, therefore, to empathize with clients who are experiencing deep and intense emotional pain (Bass & Davis, 1988).

Working with victims of sexual assault can take its toll on the counselor's physical, emotional, and spiritual well-being. Counselors are warned about the experience of secondary posttraumatic stress. Symptoms may include sleep and appetite problems, the tendency to mentally and emotionally replay the client's trauma, social withdrawal with loss of interest in sex and romance, and feelings of anxiety and loss of affect (numbing). The counselor may develop a distorted view of the world, seeing sexual assault everywhere and displaying a tendency to constantly talk about sexual abuse. Most common is a low-grade, free-floating anxiety and depression described as listlessness. The following are self-help strategies for counselors:

- Seeking supervision when a client's trauma is overwhelming to get guidance and validation about one's own responses and to share the responsibility
- Limiting talking about sexual abuse to case reviews and supervision and reserving social times for more stress-free conversation
- Actively engaging in recreational and social activities apart from working with sexual abuse survivors
- Maintaining a balance in one's caseload to avoid an overwhelming number of sexual assault survivors (Dolan, 1992)
- Developing rituals for "decompressing" and stress reduction

Rape crisis counselors whose caseloads consist entirely of sexually assaulted clients have special needs for self-maintenance. In such a setting, helping professionals are especially in need of supportive home and work environments, and they must make a very deliberate commitment to self-care and to living a healthy, balanced life outside their workplace for their own and their clients' mutual well-being.

Limit Setting in the
Counseling Relationship

The participatory treatment or intervention model, described earlier, with its commitment to a mutually respectful partnership between the counselor and client presents special issues for limit setting in the counseling relationship. Such a model inevitably blurs the distinctiveness of the counseling relationship from other kinds of relationships, including friendship, romance, or the parent/child relationship. To protect the integrity of the counselor, the client, and the relationship itself, the following must be avoided at all costs:

- Developing a romantic/sexual attachment to your client
- Having a "dual role" with a client (i.e., counseling a friend, partner, or relative)
- Allowing clients to live with you
- Discussing the client in casual conversation or breaking the rules of confidentiality in any other way

Serious consideration should be given to:

- Lending or giving money to clients
- Spending social time with clients
- Having physical contact with clients
- Giving one's home phone number to clients

All of these issues, when they arise, should be discussed in the counseling relationship and in supervision or consultation. It is also important to document the counselor's decisions and actions in questionable situations.

Caution must be exercised when considering the limits of the counseling relationship. Agencies employing counselors should develop policies and written guidelines to help counselors set appropriate boundaries and to avoid the possibility of violating their professional ethics, personal integrity, or both. Although the counseling relationship is important to the survivor's recovery, it is only one avenue for healing. Other relationships and other resources may contribute as much or more to the survivor's welfare. For this reason, strengthening the survivor's connections to her environment is an important goal for the mutual welfare of both the survivor and the counselor.

In addition to keeping her role with the survivor in perspective, the counselor must maintain a commitment to ongoing self-assessment, self-discipline, and self-care to maintain her personal health and avoid being overwhelmed by the survivor's deep needs. A key to maintaining a position of strength and to avoid being "lost" in the survivor's situation is a clear sense of one's own boundaries. Also important is the awareness that in addition to more personal emotional difficulties, the bureaucratic demands and power struggles in the helping professions frequently contribute to the helper's vulnerability to stress and burnout (Kottler, 1986).

Some recommendations for self-care and for boundary maintenance include individual counseling with a professional with whom one does not have either a personal or a professional relationship, who shares your values and beliefs, and with whom you feel a sense of trust. Therapy for the helper is advised for three reasons:

1. The counselor can experience being a client and understand the feelings of vulnerability that are part of being in the client role. As helpers we should not expect from others what we ourselves are unwilling to do.
2. Personal therapy can help the counselor look at the motivations that underlie her work as a helping professional.
3. Counseling can assist a therapist to come to terms with blind spots and any unfinished business from the past that can impinge on work with clients.

A combination of individual and group therapy can be especially helpful. More intensive personal explorations can be accomplished in individual counseling, whereas interpersonal styles and ways of relating to others can be experienced and explored in a group setting (Corey et al., 1984). Other recommendations for the counselor include positive self-talk (giving oneself the same messages that are given to clients), journaling, physical exercise, group support, and experiences of "adventure and escape" (Kottler, 1986).

Writers/therapists Anne Wilson Schaef (1986, 1992) and Jeffrey Kottler (1986) are especially confronting in their concerns about the failure of counselors to take seriously their own recovery issues. They believe that many untreated helping professionals are unaware of the addictive process in our society and frequently relate to their clients in a codependent, controlling, and dishonest way because they are out of touch with their own needs and feelings. Counselors are all too prone to self-deception, grandiosity, and perfectionism in their tendency to deny their own vulnerabilities and to avoid self-discipline and self-care. Self-maintenance is necessary to prepare to focus on the client's needs and to respond with compassion, respect, patience, self-control, and with an appreciation for the spiritual dimension to human life (Kottler, 1986).

Summary

For the counselor who is willing and available to respond to the needs of acquaintance rape survivors, effective intervention requires an adequate understanding of the problem and the recovery process, a recognition of the counselor's own limitations and vulnerabilities, and a commitment to self-knowledge and self-care. The counselor has the unique opportunity to model healthy living for the client, and the work of recovery between counselor and survivor should model a healthy relationship. The survivor must be ready for the work of recovery and willing and able to commit to the struggles and challenges that are inevitable in the healing journey.

Notes

1. Much of what has been described as feminist therapy is consistent with Ann Wilson Schaef's (1992) *living process*. Both feminist therapy and living process approaches espouse a participatory counseling relationship in which there is respect for the client's inherent strengths and inner wisdom and shared responsibility for the process and outcome of therapy.

2. The attitudes and beliefs of some church leaders could in many cases be counterproductive to the healing process and could in fact be revictimizing the victim. A response to the victim that urges silence, premature forgiveness, or both, or that assigns responsibility for the assault to the victim instead of the perpetrator increases the victim's shame and isolation and hinders her healing (Fortune, 1983). See also Chapter 8, "Revictimizing Victims," in Johnson and VanVonderen (1991).

*I don't think my life will ever be the same
as it was before I was raped.*
—An acquaintance rape survivor

10 The Survivor in the Recovery Process

The Nature of Traumatic Events

Human beings are vulnerable to a wide range of losses and hardships in the course of their lives. Such personal crises as death, divorce, relocation, sudden unemployment, and serious illness, although frequently predictable and perhaps even inevitable in people's lives, can overwhelm the victim's ability to make sense of the painful experience and to pull the pieces of a shattered life back together.

Traumatic events are distinguished from more common misfortunes by their extraordinary impact on their victims, by their possible threats to life, and by their close association with violence. Such is the case whether the threat be the force of nature in natural disasters or the force of other human beings in interpersonal violence (Herman, 1992). Assumptions about one's invulnerability and the fairness and predictability of the world may be questioned, with accompanying feelings of confusion, sadness, and despair (Janoff-Bulman, 1992). The psychophysiological changes induced by overwhelmingly stressful events are significant in their complexity and in the way they persist over time. What is common to all experiences of psychological trauma are feelings of shock, confusion, anxiety, depression, and loss of control (Gidycz & Koss, 1991).

The traumatic experience of acquaintance rape victims differs from the experience of other kinds of traumas because of the deeply personal nature of the crisis and because of the unique situational factors that affect, in a special way, the victim's appraisal of the event and her beliefs about herself (Gidycz & Koss, 1991). The special nature of acquaintance rape as a crime of violence by a known perpetrator and its distinction from stranger rape in the way it affects victims have only recently been recognized. When the harm is perpetrated by someone known to and trusted by the victim, a set of circumstances is created that is different from the harmful situations created by natural disasters or rape by a stranger. These circumstances have to do with the meaning of the rape event for the victim and with her beliefs about herself in light of the rape. Her cognitive interpretation of the rape and her self-evaluation will be primary issues in her recovery (Koss & Burkhardt, 1989). The appraisals of other persons that are often reflected in victim-blaming myths and attitudes make it difficult for a survivor to correct cognitive distortions that attribute responsibility for the rape to her failure to control the sexual situation. Evidence suggests that in relation to other types of victims, acquaintance rape victims experience more serious long-term consequences. This seems to be due to the victim's inability to recognize the event as rape and the tendency for the victim to engage in self-blame (Gidycz & Koss, 1991).

The feminist movement of the 1970s is credited with defining rape as an atrocity perpetrated against women and as a crime of violence rather than an act of sex. In those years, the shocking numbers of women victims were documented, rape crisis centers were established, and the psychological trauma of rape victims was studied and made public. The pattern of reactions to sexual assault was called the *rape trauma syndrome* and was seen to be consistent with the experiences of other trauma victims, including combat veterans. The initial focus was on street rape perpetrated by strangers. This was the first step toward shedding light on other forms of sexual violence, including acquaintance rape (Herman, 1992).

Because much of the research and writing in the 1970s about rape trauma and recovery focused on stranger rape, there was the assumption that counselors would be responding to the immediacy of a recent assault perpetrated by an unknown assailant. The rape trauma syndrome was defined as having three major phases: acute, reorganization, and resolution. In the acute phase, the person experiences shock, denial, and disbelief. She is disoriented, confused, and experiences both somatic and psychological symptoms. The emotional responses may be expressed and obvious or be more subdued and masked. In the reorganization phase, the person attempts to regain some control and self-mastery by attempting to resume relationships, work, and so on. In the resolution phase, the person begins to be able to integrate the experience as painful but one that can contribute to personal growth and maturity and to the ability to help others who have experienced similar trauma (Burgess & Holmstrom, 1979).

Since the 1970s, the problem of acquaintance rape has been recognized as a problem equally as serious as stranger rape and affecting greater numbers of persons, both male and female. Because acquaintance rape victims seldom disclose immediately after the rape (if they disclose at all), recent literature is addressing the needs of the nonrecent victim who has not been able to resolve the immediate postrape distress and who is more likely than other types of victims to develop chronic posttraumatic stress symptoms that can persist for many years (Koss & Burkhardt, 1989).

The implications of delayed disclosure or lack of disclosure are significant for the recovery process. If the victim avoids or delays disclosure, the benefits of early intervention to relieve traumatic symptoms, provide medical attention, and assist with making legal decisions are lost. This means that victims are not able to move through the recovery phases and are vulnerable to getting stuck in the acute or disorganization phase with symptoms of anxiety and depression that become chronic and persistently debilitating. It is not unusual for victims of past acquaintance rapes to seek mental health services with problems that are, in reality, the symptoms of unresolved sexual abuse trauma.[1] Also, if the disclosure is delayed, revictimization is more likely to occur. Lingering and persistent traumatic symptoms make it difficult for the person to have the psychological resources for self-protection from further abuse. Because acquaintance rape victims are less likely to conceptualize the event as rape and more likely to assume responsibility for the rape, they are vulnerable to revictimization by the same person as well as by other perpetrators. Repeated victimization, including early childhood trauma, has a cumulative effect, seriously complicates the recovery process, and is recognized as a strong factor in the development of long-term mental health problems (Gidycz & Koss, 1991).

The pattern of symptoms known as the rape trauma syndrome and the impact of the rape trauma will vary according to the circumstances of the rape, the characteristics of the perpetrator and victim, and the response of other people in the victim's life. Essential features of the rape trauma that persist over time may be seen in any of the following ways:

- Fear/avoidance responses manifested as phobic and panic attacks
- Depressed mood ranging from moderate to severe with the risk for suicide
- Diminished self-esteem with feelings of shame and worthlessness
- A sense of helplessness and powerlessness
- Addictions
- The inability to sustain close relationships
- A loss of interest in sexual intimacy or sexual acting out
- Sleep and eating disorders
- Persistent somatic complaints, most typically headaches, backaches, and gastrointestinal problems (Gidycz & Koss, 1991)[2]

To define integration and resolution is to define the goals for the intervention process. It is to view the end of the healing journey and the culmination of the work of recovery. Following is a checklist for recovery that incorporates recommendations from various sources for defining the expectations for integration and resolution of rape trauma:

- Anxiety is mastered; major phobias and panic attacks are diminished.
- The victim is able to recall the experience without reliving it.

- Responsibility for the rape is appropriately attributed to the perpetrator.

- There is orientation to the present and future rather than the past.

- There is motivation and energy to carry out life tasks and responsibilities, including work and personal relationships.

- Evidence is available of a more positive self-concept and more assertive behavior to protect against further victimization.

- Fewer stereotypical attitudes and beliefs about male/female behaviors are evident.

- The ability is present to interpret the rape event as an experience that forces growth and maturity with new insights and new feelings of strength and self-mastery.

- The rape is seen as a consciousness-raising experience and a challenge to overcome. (Gidycz & Koss, 1991; Janoff-Bulman, 1992; Koss & Burkhardt, 1989)

The Work of Recovery

The work of recovery for the counselor and survivor is to effectively integrate the rape experience into the survivor's memories of the past and into the meaning and purpose of her life in the present and future. The use of the term *recovery* is somewhat misleading because to recover is to imply returning to a previous state. Rape victims, however, in the process of disclosing and integrating their victimization can never return to where they were before the trauma. It is hoped that as they heal they will regain and perhaps surpass a previous level of functioning as they gain new insights and build more mature and realistic assumptions about themselves, other people, and the world. However, they will never be the same (Janoff-Bulman, 1992). Although we use the term recovery as preferable to *treatment*, we use it interchangeably with *healing* as words that best describe the victim's journey to survivorship and wholeness.

The work of recovery includes careful assessment and skillful interventions. Knowing who the victim is and what has happened to her are the essential factors for assessment and require that the counselor provide the emotional safety for accurate and complete data gathering. A comprehensive assessment will define the nature of the survivor's needs and the interventions that will best meet those needs.

Issues for Assessment

To effectively "be with" an acquaintance rape victim and to assist her on the road to recovery, the counselor must have a reservoir of knowledge and skills to draw from; accurate insight into her own values, beliefs, and vulnerabilities concerning sexual victimization; and the ability to assess and respond to the victim and her situation (Laidlaw et al., 1990). A dual focus on both the survivor and her circumstances cannot be too strongly emphasized because every psychosocial problem represents a dynamic relationship between the person and her environment (Strean, 1985). When presented with a request for help from an acquaintance rape victim, the helper will be prepared to collect and assess information that is essential to planning effective interventions. Data gathering is "looking at" the survivor and her circumstances; assessment is "thinking about" or reflecting on who the victim is, what are the circumstances of her victimization, and what interventions and resources may be needed (Strean, 1985). Such information will focus on the victim (gender, age, relationship to the perpetrator, and pre-rape functioning including previous victimization) and the circumstances of the rape and of disclosure (use of alcohol by the victim, the perpetrator, or both; number of assailants; degree of degradation and violence; and response of significant others). Careful attention must be given to the data-gathering/assessment process because a careful and skillful assessment builds a solid foundation for an effective intervention and recovery process.

Who Is the Victim?

Gender

Although this book is focused primarily on female acquaintance rape victims, we recognize that males, too, can be subjected to forced

sex. Differentiating between the responses of male and female victims will help the counselor to understand the way females and
males attach different meanings to the assault as reflected in the
following comments of female and male survivors:

Rape makes you feel dirty and cheap. (female survivor)

An older guy forced sex on me when I was sixteen. Is that rape?
What kind of a guy gets raped? (male survivor)

As stated earlier in this book, victims of rape are observed in all
socioeconomic levels, all age groups, and in both sexes. Victims
share common characteristics in their response to their sexual assault trauma, with both males and females manifesting symptoms
of depression, anxiety, somatic disorders, and sexual dysfunctioning. Males and females will, however, assign different meanings to
their victimization. Females are likely to attach moral significance
to the rape, with a sense of being morally corrupted and becoming
"damaged goods." Special trauma is associated with women who
report the rape as their first experience of intercourse because of the
identification of victimization with sexual intimacy and the accompanying feelings of powerlessness, betrayal, and shame. The counselor, at some point in the recovery process, may need to help the
survivor distinguish between biological virginity and psychological
virginity (Parrot, 1988a).

Males typically experience rape as an assault on their gender
identity and feel a loss of masculinity whether the rape is perpetrated by another male or by a female. Whereas a woman may feel
"stupid" and "bad" for not being able to resist forced sex, a man may
feel "not enough of a man" or "weak" for not preventing the sexual
encounter, for not being in control of the situation, or both. He may
subsequently become very physically, verbally, or sexually aggressive to prove his manhood (Janoff-Bulman, 1992; King, 1992; Parrot,
1988a; Struckman-Johnson, 1991).

A prime recovery issue in both homosexual- and female-perpe-
trated sexual victimization is the recognition that stereotypical
expectations for female passivity and male dominance are contra-

dicted. This presents special problems for help seeking and for accurately appraising the nature of the assault and its meaning for the victim. Effective interventions with female survivors will focus primarily on restoring a sense of self-worth. With male survivors, the primary issue is the restoration of confidence in his masculine self.

Age

The victim's age is another significant variable in data gathering and assessment.

> The rape was my first sexual experience. I sort of went crazy after that and got real promiscuous. Nobody knew why. I was 13 then and I'm 30 now. I still feel like a bad girl.

Because the highest numbers of acquaintance rapes are seen in the 17 to 26 age group, the majority of female acquaintance rape victims are among adolescents and young adults. This means that the rape occurs in the midst of life tasks that are related to establishing a sense of identity. Sexual trauma is especially significant during early adolescence because young people are forming their understanding of themselves, the world, and their view of male/female relationships (Burkhardt, 1991).

The experience of trauma tends to fixate young victims at one point in their psychosocial growth. They are prevented by this fixation from moving through the remainder of their development. Their sense of identity becomes fused with and shaped by the sexual victimization and they easily adopt a victim mentality that is highly sexualized. Adolescents are typically blamed and labeled as promiscuous or incorrigible for behaviors that are the predictable consequences of sexual victimization. Adults with a history of child or adolescent sexual trauma often behave socially and sexually immature. They have great difficulty maintaining personal boundaries and sustaining close, long-term relationships. Like adolescent victims, they may lack impulse control in sexual or social relationships or they may remain sexually and socially isolated and withdrawn.

Age-related recovery issues include the following:

- Developing a healthy self-concept that is based on one's intrinsic worth and value instead of on the rape event or other past abuses
- Recovering lost stages of development with healthy nonsexual relationships with both sexes
- Healing and integrating the sexual self for a more completely developed sense of identity (Blume, 1990)[3]

Relationship to the Perpetrator

The relationship between the victim and perpetrator is another important concern for the counselor.

> I didn't think it was rape because it happened with my brother-in-law. I didn't tell anyone for 10 years. I was depressed all the time because I blamed myself and felt so guilty.

Unlike the experience of stranger rape, acquaintance rape means that someone known to and trusted by the victim has violated and betrayed her in the most intimate and personal way possible. Studies that compare the impact of stranger versus nonstranger rape indicate that familiarity between the victim and perpetrator is a significant factor in the victim's inability to acknowledge the rape and to successfully recover. When compared with women raped by strangers, women raped by nonstrangers blamed themselves more for the rape, saw themselves in a less positive light, and over a similar period of time felt less recovered from the rape (Katz, 1991).

Evidence suggests that acquaintance rape victims experience a psychological "double bind." The victim experiences the traumatic experience as rape, but unlike rape by a stranger, neither she nor society can name what happened to her as rape. Consequently, she must act as if the rape has not happened or is not real. Also, because she has been socialized to take care of men and to accommodate their needs, she is not prepared to be self-protecting and wary of men. But that very prescription for what she is supposed to do and be becomes the instrument of her victimization and another double bind (Burkhardt, 1991). Because of her familiarity with the perpetrator and the resulting confusion about what constitutes rape, acquaintance rape victims are less likely to name the experience as rape, less likely to disclose and report, and less likely to effectively integrate and resolve the trauma (Katz, 1991).

Typically, the more bonded the relationship between the victim and perpetrator, the deeper and more lasting the trauma. More important than how long the victim has known the perpetrator is the *meaning* of the relationship for her, the level of trust, and the extent to which her sense of identity and self-worth are affected by the relationship (Katz, 1991). Also significant is her vulnerability to the position of power the perpetrator has in her life. A person who is sexually violated by a priest or minister is likely to experience a unique kind of trauma because of the serious breach of trust with spiritual as well as psychosocial consequences (Fortune, 1989). The relationship between victim and perpetrator will significantly affect the responses of other people who know both parties and may feel loyalties to both the victim and the perpetrator. They may become aligned with the perpetrator and blame the victim in their efforts to avoid and deny the rape. In the minds of many, if the victim can be blamed for the rape, then there is no rape. Such victim blaming and rape denying is typically seen in families, churches, workplaces, and on college campuses. Issues for recovery focus on the meaning of the relationship for the victim, loss of trust, attribution of responsibility for the rape, and the response of significant others.

Pre-Rape Functioning, Including Previous Victimization

As the following quotation from an acquaintance rape survivor indicates, pre-rape functioning and especially previous sexual victimization are important assessment issues for the counselor.

Those of us who have suffered childhood abuse are perfectly set up for acquaintance rape. We have no boundaries or sense of personal rights to our bodies. One of my greatest difficulties now, after nearly 3 years of therapy, is being willing to claim my body as part of me and take care of it.

Whether or not the victim has experienced sexual assault for the first time is significant for the recovery process because of the meaning of the rape for the victim and because of the implications for further victimization. The first-time or single-incident victim is likely to experience a shattering of her belief system and her views of herself and the world. Having never been a victim before, she is likely to have perceived herself as invulnerable, with a sense of goodness and personal power. She may have assumed, consciously or unconsciously, that rape is something that happens to other people who are not as good or who are irresponsible or foolish. To reconcile what has happened to her with her assumptions, she concludes that either what happened was not rape, that it was not so bad, or that it was her fault and *she* is bad (Janoff-Bulman, 1992).

Multiple-rape victims appear to be more at risk for a delayed response. This indicates stronger psychological defenses against the reality of the rape and greater efforts to deny the assault. These defenses are protective mechanisms established over time. For this reason, the victim of multiple assaults will appear to be coping well. She convinces herself and others that she is doing well. The delayed response is, in fact, a symptom of the victim's effort to deny and control the impact of the assault. The victim is likely to report the assault with little emotion and perhaps in a matter-of-fact manner. She may not be able to identify and report the symptoms she is experiencing. This can be deceiving for the untrained and inexperienced counselor who may see the response as indifference or as good coping. The skillful helper will be able to recognize and interpret the delayed response as a symptom of denial and as a defense mechanism (Marhoefer-Dvorak, Resick, Hutter, & Girelli, 1988).

Multiple victimization creates special long-term mental and emotional stress. Multiple-rape victims report significantly more problems than single-rape victims in social and sexual functioning, in feelings of paranoia and anger, in suicidal thoughts and behaviors, and in the need for psychiatric treatment (Marhoefer-Dvorak et al., 1988). In addition to prior victimization, other aspects of pre-rape functioning are important factors in the victim's recovery process, including such life stressors as insufficient financial resources, lack of social support, chronic health problems, and prior losses due to death or divorce.

Poor pre-rape functioning and prior victimization are seen as increasing an individual's vulnerability to further victimization. Survivors of child sexual abuse are more likely to develop low self-esteem, social isolation, depression, and substance abuse and are subsequently more likely to become victims of other forms of sexual victimization, including acquaintance rape (Harney & Muelenhard, 1991).

Vulnerability to victimization, however, must be distinguished from responsibility for victimization. When a person has been repeatedly victimized, she comes to expect to be sexually assaulted. She believes she has no alternative but to submit to further victimization. She submits, but she does not consent, because to consent is to willingly choose. The person who has been victimized repeatedly does not know that she has the right to choose whether or not to engage in sexual activity, nor does she feel confident that her choice would be respected. She submits. Each victimization tells her again that she is powerless to choose and that she has no worth or value as a human being. Multiple victimization is often mistakenly seen as a self-destructive wish for continued abuse. Rather, it is symptomatic of a history that predisposes the individual to compulsively continue being abused, a history that began long before the person could choose or understand what was happening to her (Blume, 1990). Women who have experienced a history of sexual abuse and other forms of mistreatment usually lack a clear sense of personal boundaries and have difficulty asserting themselves and setting limits—issues that must be discussed in the recovery process. Such victims may not be able to accurately interpret social cues because of their distorted understanding of interpersonal relationships. Their sense of themselves as worthless or irreparably damaged increases their vulnerability to further victimization (Katz, 1991).

Thus, issues for assessment include the belief system of the first-time victim and the extent of her assumed invulnerability, the nature of pre-rape functioning and possible previous victimization, defense mechanisms employed by the victim, and the impact of sexual assault on psychosocial functioning and self-esteem.

What Were the Circumstances
of the Rape and of the Disclosure?

Use of Alcohol, Drugs, or Pornography

The use of alcohol, drugs, or pornography are variables the counselor must take into account in assessment.

> We both had a few drinks. We watched some movies. I didn't realize what was happening until things had gone too far and I couldn't stop it. I was raped, but I blame myself.

Alcohol, drugs, and pornography play significant roles in modern dating rituals. Alcohol and drugs are expected at social functions, and their use is known to reduce inhibitions and impair judgment with the result that both victims and perpetrators of acquaintance rape engage in behaviors that are high risk and impulsive. Many college males routinely use alcohol to break down a woman's resistance to sexual activity. When the use of drugs or alcohol has been a factor in the rape situation, the perpetrator is seen as less blameworthy and the victim seen as more blameworthy (Richardson & Hammock, 1991).

The use of pornography is becoming more prevalent with the availability of X-rated videos. Pornography acts as a disinhibitor to sexual aggression by supporting rape myths and by portraying forced sex as erotic and enjoyable to the victim. The widespread availability and use of pornographic movies and literature appears to contribute to a climate of acceptance for depersonalized sex and interpersonal violence (Harney & Muehlenhard, 1991; Rapport & Posey, 1991).

When acquaintance rape occurs, social rituals in which the victim has participated serve to confuse the issue of her victimization and tend to assign blame to the victim who "should have known better." In cases of acquaintance rape where both the perpetrator and victim have used substances, pornography, or both, interventions should focus on helping the survivor to accurately appraise the rape by distinguishing the unwanted, forced sex that was not her fault from the high-risk activity that may have been unwise and that she may or may not have willingly participated in. In such cases, it is important to help the victim distinguish *submission* to forced sex from *consent* to forced sex.

Single or Multiple Perpetrators

The number of perpetrators can affect the path to recovery the counselor takes with the victim.

> It was horrible. I had terrible nightmares, didn't go to class, withdrew from all of my friends. I was so afraid someone would find out that 6 guys had sex with me that night. My boyfriend broke up with me. I don't think I'll ever be able to be close to a guy again.

Victimization by a single perpetrator is considered to be the usual and predictable acquaintance rape scenario. Whatever force and humiliation occur in a one-on-one rape incident, the incident is typically private and less prone to public acts of humiliation and degradation. Unless the perpetrator chooses to divulge his offense, the victim has some control over who learns about the rape.

Circumstances are different in cases of multiple perpetrators or "gang rape." Groups of males banding together and engaging in violent and degrading sexual acts with female victims has until recently been seen as isolated incidences that occur infrequently in exceptional circumstances. The media is now documenting that gang rape is more common than was once supposed. Women are frequent victims of such crimes, especially on college campuses where sexual victimization is often viewed as "party games" and where in fraternities disinhibited sexual activity is perpetrated by a climate of acceptance.

Major issues for intervention include the public nature of the victimization, consequent humiliation, loss of self-esteem, and increased traumatic consequences for the victim due to the violence and degradation that are often characteristic of gang acquaintance rapes. Victims typically do not report incidences of gang rape with acquaintances and will suffer in silence to avoid further exposure and embarrassment. Because most gang rapes go unreported, colleges and universities often assume such rapes do not occur. Such denial may in fact encourage the practice to continue unabated and to work against victims seeking help and perpetrators being apprehended. Campus administrators must engage in aggressive education and prevention programs, particularly with fraternities and sororities, to create a safe and supportive environment for victims to disclose, seek legal redress, and to receive counseling without humiliation or blame (Ehrhart & Sandler, 1985).

Degree of Violence and Degradation

Although violence is generally associated primarily with stranger rape, violence as well as degradation can occur in the context of acquaintance rape, as the following quotation from an acquaintance rape survivor indicates:

> He had a razor blade. He threatened to cut me. I was terrified. I was forced to perform oral sex over and over again. I felt like a thing, an object. It's still hard for me to feel like a human being. I sometimes feel like I'm watching myself and am not in my body.

The circumstances in which acquaintance rape occurs varies widely from intimate, private sex by force perpetrated by subtle entrapment and coercion to single or multiple offenders perpetrating unspeakable acts of aggression and degradation with mutilation and the threat of death. In some cases, actual deaths do occur. The circumstances of the rape will be a primary issue for assessing the nature and extent of the trauma and the meaning of the rape for the victim.

Generally, the greater the degree of violence, the greater the fear response and the more intense the symptoms of posttraumatic stress disorder. Lesser violence and more subtle forms of victimization are likely to create more confusion in the victim and more tendency to deny the reality of the rape because of self-blame, anxiety about what the rapist might be thinking or feeling, and society's failure to view acquaintance rape as rape (Parrot, 1991).

Circumstances of Disclosure

Disclosure is a risk for most victims. The victim takes the chance of not being believed or taken seriously, of being blamed and judged, of feeling less safe and trusting than she felt before she told anyone. Nearly one half of all women raped by male acquaintances never tell anyone and only 5% report to authorities (Warshaw, 1988).

> I didn't make a police report or go to the hospital. I didn't think anyone would believe that I was raped by someone I knew. I didn't want to feel like a victim again. Three months later I found out I was pregnant.

Interpersonal violence, by its very nature, works against victim disclosure. Although human beings find it easy to sympathize with victims of natural disaster, they find it more difficult to believe and support a victim of violence perpetrated by an acquaintance. The victim of a known offender is "suspect" and is seen to be in some way responsible for her victimization or to be lying or exaggerating the assault. In many cases of acquaintance rape, the loyalties of friends and family members are divided between the victim and perpetrator. It is not unusual for everyone in the victim's life to be aligned with the perpetrator who predictably promotes denial and silence. If this fails, the perpetrator attacks the victim's credibility. Other persons who for their own reasons prefer silence and denial will participate in the protection of the perpetrator.

When the victim discloses, she asks other persons to be witnesses —to believe and accept the reality of her victimization and to share her pain. To be a witness to the victim's painful realities is to give time and energy to assisting her in recovery. To be a witness also means to advocate for her rights and her needs. Such a commitment is usually accepted reluctantly, if at all, by friends, family members, or by the general public who would prefer to be bystanders and who may eventually even become her accusers (Herman, 1992). The counselor then is often in the position of being the only support available to the victim and must in many cases work with the survivor to expand her social network and her supportive connection to the environment.

Interventions for Recovery

Data gathering and assessment occur in the early stages of counseling and continue throughout recovery as new information emerges to inform and guide the interventions. Another major consideration in the recovery process is the intervention strategies and modalities that promote healing from rape trauma. Essential to the effectiveness of interventions, however, is the counselor's orientation and approach to her work and to the survivor's needs. As discussed in the previous chapter, this book promotes a collaborative approach to intervention. In this model the counselor is a companion and advocate to the survivor. The counselor brings knowledge and skills to the counseling relationship to facilitate and guide the work of recovery. The survivor is seen as the expert about what is at issue and what helps. The counselor is prepared to openly disclose her values and orientation and to thereby demystify her therapeutic role. This demystification serves to diminish the power imbalance between counselor and client. Such a mutually respectful helping relationship works to promote the trust and safety the survivor needs to embark on her healing journey (Laidlaw et al., 1990).

Crisis Intervention
With the Recent Victim

A careful and skillful assessment and a client-centered orientation to intervention will provide a reliable basis for determining what the victim needs. A basic assumption of the authors is that knowing how to help an acquaintance rape victim is essential for everyone, as essential as knowing any other first aid (Warshaw, 1988).

Because victims will disclose when and with whom they feel sufficient emotional safety, and because they may disclose immediately after a rape if that safety is available, anyone in the victim's social network, including friends, parents, relatives, and spouses, may be in a position of responding to a request for help. A model for acquaintance rape "first aid" is presented in Box 10.1. We believe that all of the essential elements of effective crisis intervention are

BOX 10.1

What to Do

Here are 14 guidelines that counseling experts advise for helping someone you know recover from acquaintance rape.

1. *Believe her.* The greatest fear of acquaintance rape survivors is that they will not be believed, or that their experience will be minimized as "not important." Women are raped by men they know *four times more often* than by strangers. Accept what you are hearing—even if the man involved is a popular, desirable guy, even if the woman appears confused and unable to put her thoughts together clearly. She is in shock. She may also seem calm and collected, behavior that may seem inappropriate in someone who has just been raped. Both extremes are possible (and normal) reactions.

Attempted rape is often as traumatic as completed rape. Although the woman may have foiled the rape or the man may have been unable to penetrate her, the aftereffects of the experience may be severe. Treat the victim of attempted rape with the same care as the victim of completed rape.

2. *Listen.* Find somewhere to be alone with the woman and just let her talk. She may not begin in a rush of words, so be patient. Let her know that listening to her is more important then anything else she may think you want to do. Let her tell the story at her own speed.

3. *Comfort her.* Try to calm her down if she's agitated, but do so in a soothing—not disapproving—way. She may want to be held while she cries or may not want to be touched. Offer tea, cocoa, soup, a blanket, a stuffed animal. One date rape victim recalls her friend giving her a flannel nightgown. These suggestions all give the woman a warm, secure feeling in sharp contrast to what she has just experienced.

4. *Reinforce that the rape was not her fault.* Avoid questions that seem to blame her for her actions, such as "Why didn't you scream?" and

"Why did you go to his room?" Allow her to talk out her feelings of self-blame, if she wants to, but make her see that the rapist caused the rape, not her.

5. *Provide protection.* Give her a secure place to sleep and companionship once she returns to her own living quarters. If she lives alone, strongly recommend that you stay with her for at least one night.

6. *Suggest calling a rape crisis center.* This does not mean that the woman must report the rape to police. A rape crisis center will provide a trained worker to guide the survivor (and her friend) through the next critical hours. All calls to rape crisis hot lines are confidential. To find one in your community, look under "Rape" in the white pages of the telephone directory. This is an important step to take even if the woman has not yet attached the word "rape" to her experience.

7. *Encourage her to preserve evidence.* The sooner an acquaintance rape is reported, the better the likelihood of charges being filed and the offender being convicted. However, because so many women fail to recognize their experience as rape until days, weeks, months, and even years later, vital evidence is lost. Call a rape crisis hot line and get information about having the woman undergo a post-rape examination *before* she washes her hands, face, and body or brushes her teeth. During an official rape exam in a hospital, specimens will be taken from her to find traces of blood, hair, saliva, and semen from the rapist, so it is important that nothing be washed away. The woman may change her clothes if she puts all the clothing she was wearing during the assault in paper bags (a separate bag for each article so specimens do not become contaminated).

8. *Treat her medical needs.* She may have bruises, cuts, or other injuries. Even if she appears unhurt, encourage her to get medical attention. She should receive treatment because the rapist may have had a sexually transmitted disease or she might become pregnant from the rape. Go with her to the hospital, clinic, or doctor's office and stay during the examination if she wants.

9. *Help her organize her thoughts, but let her make decisions about how to proceed.* The acquaintance rape survivor needs to regain the feeling

of being in control. Allow her to do that. Parents of a raped teenager may want to press charges, but that might not be the best choice for their child. Likewise, friends of an older woman might want to arrest the man involved. Try to separate how you feel about what has happened from what is best for the woman's recovery. If she decides not to report it and you disagree with that, let her know that you support her decision nonetheless.

10. *If you are her lover, with her approval, use appropriate touching and language to reestablish her feelings of worth.* Gently touching will help her understand that your connection with her is unbroken, that you do not consider her "dirty." Let her decide when sexual activity and intercourse should begin again. Do not pressure her out of the belief that you need to prove everything is "normal" between you. Some victims have sex again before they are ready just to allay partners' fears about becoming sexual again.

11. *Help her get psychological and legal help.* In the immediate aftermath of acquaintance rape, the survivor may not be able to seek out sources for help. Do the legwork for her. Drive her to appointments or baby-sit or provide other help so she can meet with lawyers, police, and counselors.

12. *Be available.* In the weeks and months following the rape, reassure the woman that she can turn to you whenever she needs to. Then, when she does, give her your time and attention.

13. *Learn about rape trauma syndrome.* Your friend's recovery period will last a long time, during which her moods and reactions may change radically from one day to the next.

14. *Get help for yourself.* You need to talk with someone other than the acquaintance rape survivor to discuss your feelings about the attack and its aftermath. A rape crisis center, women's center, or university counseling center will be able to suggest someone who can help you.

SOURCE: 14 Guidelines from pages 181-184 in *I Never Called It Rape* by Robin Warshaw. Copyright © 1988 by The Ms. Foundation for Education and Communication, Inc. and Sarah Lazin Books. Reprinted by permission of HarperCollins Publishers, Inc.

included in this formulation. It is assumed that this information can be used by anyone, professional or nonprofessional, who is in a helping position with a recent acquaintance rape victim.

Interventions With
the Nonrecent Victim

Because research indicates that only a small percentage of acquaintance rape victims seek help immediately after the rape, counselors must be prepared to meet the needs of the "nonrecent" victim (Koss & Burkhardt, 1989). These needs are seen to be unique because the nonrecent victim who has been raped by an acquaintance cognitively interprets the rape event in a way that perpetuates shame and self-blame and prolongs and inhibits recovery.

Because much of the rape recovery literature has focused primarily on the recent victim, the focus of the remainder of this chapter will be on the postacquaintance rape trauma that is not resolved, that persists in a chronic pattern over time, and that has serious long-term implications for the psychosocial well-being of survivors (Katz, 1991).

Theories and approaches to counseling that support the interventions discussed here include the following:

- Systems theory that sees the survivor in her situation and is concerned with the dynamic interaction between the survivor and her environment (Strean, 1985)

- Cognitive restructuring to meet the needs of the nonrecent victim to name the rape, correct distortions that perpetrate self-blame, and find meaning in her experiences (Koss & Burkhardt, 1989)

- Solution-focused interventions that make use of the survivor's own resources for recovery and empowers the survivor to define and carry out her own solutions for change (Dolan, 1991)

- Feminist theory that provides an overall framework for client-centered intervention for promoting self-expression, self-valuing, and self-mastery

Stages of Recovery
for the Nonrecent Victim

Three primary stages constitute the path to recovery that the counselor and victim traverse. They are the following:

1. Crisis stabilization and the establishment of an emotionally safe environment for the work of recovery
2. Reconstructing and reframing the trauma story with interventions that diminish the stress and anxiety and that correct cognitive distortions
3. Restoring the connections between the survivor and her environment with solutions that are present- and future-oriented and that provide a sense of hope and meaning (Herman, 1992)

Crisis Stabilization and Establishing
an Emotionally Safe Environment

The quality of the relationship in the counseling process is essential to the safety the survivor must feel in order to heal. Without the assurance of safety and trust, the survivor will feel revictimized by the response of the counselor if that response is in any way cold, distancing, judgmental, or blaming. If the counselor tends to deny or diminish the victim's rape experience, the survivor's safety will be in jeopardy.

The counselor/client relationship is in all cases vulnerable to issues of power and control, issues that become more crucial and more significant in the rape counseling experience. In cases of acquaintance rape, the survivor has experienced an extreme and deeply personal loss of power and control. If she reexperiences being controlled and manipulated by a counselor, she will feel violated and victimized again by someone in a position of trust. For this reason, the counselor's beliefs, attitudes, and skills are essential to the survivor's feelings of safety and to her eventual recovery.

A primary commitment from the counselor, therefore, is to empower the survivor and to support her in her efforts to become autonomous and strong, with the ability to make choices that are self-protecting and life enhancing. There may be situations, however, when the survivor is at risk to self-harm or harm from others and when the counselor must assume responsibility for the survivor's safety. Even in these cases, however, when the victim is for the time being unable to be self-protecting, the counselor should consult with the client and provide as much opportunity as possible for the client to make decisions for herself (Herman, 1992).

In every case the counselor will be motivated to respond based on the survivor's need for physical and emotional safety with the goal of empowering her for self-mastery and self-determination. The counselor should consistently communicate empathy with the client's experience and insightful understanding of the client's needs.

Reconstructing and Reframing the Trauma Story

Acquaintance rape victims, like victims of other traumatic events, experience flashbacks (sudden reliving of the event), nightmares, and intrusive thoughts in their efforts to complete the cognitive processing and to psychologically assimilate and integrate the event. This completion process, seen as necessary and as an essential part of the healing process is, however, accompanied by physical and emotional arousal that can become intolerable and persistent without intervention that externalizes the trauma and provides relief and resolution. The client can experience difficulties that can be manifested as panic attacks, phobias, addictions, obsessive-compulsive disorders, and serious suicidal depression. Relief from these traumatic symptoms ultimately is found in disclosure and talking about the event. The benefits of externalizing the trauma verbally, either by talking or in writing, are seen to be both physiologically and cognitively beneficial. Translating the experience from memory to language reduces the need to repeatedly relive the event and to reexperience again and again the associated trauma. Symptoms are seen as attempts to gain some control and self-mastery over memories and feelings that overwhelm the survivor's ability to process and integrate the victimizing memory (Janoff-Bulman, 1992). Active and verbal processing of the experience can help the survivor accomplish healthy mastery of the trauma.

Talking about rape and externalizing the trauma, however, is not enough. Also essential to the recovery process for the victim is the opportunity to confront and correct cognitive distortions associated with the acquaintance rape experience that perpetuate feelings of shame and self-blame. The counselor must be prepared to help the survivor reappraise the rape event in a way that helps the victim experience "fit" with her understanding of herself and the world (Janoff-Bulman, 1992). The recovery concerns in the reconstruction/ reframing process include the following:

- Pacing
- Reduction of stressful psycho-physiological symptoms
- Reframing the event to diminish the survivor's self-blame and enhance her self-esteem and self-mastery

In pacing the process of disclosure and recalling the rape, the survivor typically displays approach/avoidance responses. When she is approaching the trauma, she is talking about and reliving the rape with accompanying feelings of anxiety with nightmares, flashbacks, and panic attacks. When she is avoiding the trauma, she is withdrawn, numb, and likely to be feeling depressed and "shut down." The counselor will be able to recognize the "dialectic" and pace the work of recovery in tandem with the responses of the survivor and with her approach/avoidance pattern, providing strategies that prevent the survivor from constantly approaching or constantly avoiding the trauma (Janoff-Bulman, 1992). In addition, the survivor will alternate periods of active self-expression and "work" with periods of retreat and rest when maintenance and supportive counseling are most helpful. An overly expressive intervention approach, or encouraging the survivor to recall and relive the trauma over and over, can be viewed as revictimization. Pacing will help the survivor to feel supported and understood by the counselor and will empower her to feel that the process is being guided by the survivor's needs and not by the counselor's expectations.

The client should be reassured that painful traumatic symptoms such as nightmares, flashbacks, and intrusive thoughts are normal in the early stages of recovery and that talking about the rape and her feelings about what happened will bring relief over time. In addition to talking, other forms of self-expression can be helpful to the stabilization process such as writing, drawing, and guided imagery exercises. Solution-focused interventions help to modify symptoms of anxiety and depression by anchoring the survivor to the present and asking her to identify behaviors that will indicate that she is feeling, thinking, and acting less like a victim and more like a survivor. The goal is to help the survivor to recall the rape event without constantly reliving it and to be oriented to the present and future instead of the past (Dolan, 1991).[4] In addition, the counselor should be prepared to evaluate the level of anxiety and depression and determine when medication may be helpful or necessary and to make a medical referral. Symptom relief with medication in combination with expressive therapy is often the most effective and efficient intervention strategy for trauma survivors.

As previously indicated, the rape treatment literature available until recently focused on the recent victim and on alleviating affective symptoms of anxiety and depression. There is now the recognition that nonrecent victims require a more cognitive approach to intervention (Gidycz & Koss, 1991). The counselor assumes three primary tasks in helping the survivor to reappraise and reframe the rape experience.

First, the counselor can help the survivor to appraise the rape in a way that attributes responsibility for the rape to the perpetrator and diminishes her self-blame. However unwise her behaviors in the situation, the survivor should know that nothing she said or did justified being subjected to sex against her will. In an effort, however, to prevent further victimization, the counselor can, in a sensitive and nonblaming way, help the survivor to recognize how she may have put herself at risk by not being sufficiently self-valuing and self-protecting.

Second, the counselor should provide positive mirroring to enhance the survivor's self-esteem and self-confidence. The counselor can also help the survivor develop a more mature understanding of the world, with the knowledge that as human beings all of us are vulnerable to pain and loss but that with our own inner strengths and the help of others we can overcome painful experiences and make them a meaningful part of our lives. It is important for the survivor to recognize that the rape need not define who she is or the kind of person she wants to be. Survivors can find meaning and purpose in having survived and recovered from the rape, with new insights and wisdom that will prepare them to be advocates and witnesses for others (Herman, 1992).

Third, the counselor can strengthen the survivor's feelings of self-mastery by helping her to adopt less stereotypical thinking about male/female relationships and to act more assertively and more self-protecting. Preventive education about the dynamics of male/female relationships and about acquaintance rape can empower the survivor to develop relationships of equality and respect.

Restoring Connection to the Survivor's Environment

Throughout the recovery process, from the initial disclosure through stabilization and reframing to termination, there will be a recognition of the need to reduce the survivor's isolation and to facilitate her connections to the present and future and to other persons and resources. These connections, that are essential in the early stages of recovery to help the survivor avoid being consumed by and identified with the rape experience, are facilitated by interventions that create feelings of safety and helpfulness (Herman, 1992).

Staying connected to the present and future enables the survivor to carry out life tasks and to sustain relationships with other people. The helper who approaches her work with a person-in-situation perspective is able to intervene in other systems on behalf of the survivor and to link her to resources that are beyond the capacity of the helper and her agency to provide. An additional commitment from the counselor is to assist the survivor in restoring and maintaining significant relationships that have been negatively affected by the survivor's experience as a victim.

The psychosocial costs of acquaintance rape are significant with long-term consequences for victims, perpetrators, families, communities, and for society as a whole. Along with the costs to mental and emotional health, there are job loss and absenteeism, school failure, addictive behaviors that are self-defeating and self-destructive, and family and marital breakdown. The work of helping the survivor to restore and sustain connections typically includes the following:

1. Intervening in other systems will help prevent losses that will result in further disempowerment for the survivor. This may mean, for example, contacts with teachers, supervisors, medical personnel, court officials, and social service agencies to advocate for the survivor's special needs.

2. Intervening with family members, friends, and/or spouses will help significant others to accurately and appropriately appraise and interpret the rape and to support and provide safety for the survivor. Special interventions are often required with the survivor's father, husband, or boyfriend who are likely to display stereotypical responses to the rape. Such responses are seen in behaviors and attitudes that are either overly protective and controlling, overly blaming and angry, or overly distancing and rejecting. These responses intensify the survivor's feelings of helplessness, shame, and isolation. If, on the other hand, the important males in her life can be understanding and supportive, they can play a significant role in facilitating her recovery and restoring a sense of trust in men. (Ledray, 1986)[5]

3. It is helpful to link the survivor to a support group that deals specifically with the issue of acquaintance rape and that helps to validate the reality of her experience and to affirm her as a person. A support group is especially important when significant others do not understand the survivor's experience or when the survivor is unable to share her experience with friends or family members. (Janoff-Bulman, 1992)[6]

Important to the ability to restore and sustain healthy connections to one's environment is an orientation to the future that is positive and hopeful, with a capacity to relate to others in a healthy way and to see one's life as meaningful and purposeful. To see possibilities for personal growth in the rape recovery process and to be able to integrate the experience into a healthy and positive view of oneself is the ultimate experience of recovery (Janoff-Bulman, 1992).

Interventions for Complex
Posttraumatic Stress Disorder

The rape counseling material presented thus far assumes that the survivor's presenting problem is the acquaintance rape and that what she needs is an emotionally safe environment to disclose and talk about the rape experience, information to correct cognitive distortions and reorder her assumptions, and help with reconnecting with relationships in her life and with her life task. It is further assumed that she will have the mental and emotional sturdiness to make the recovery journey and to eventually integrate the experience into her total self with more wisdom and strength for having gone through the recovery experience.

These assumptions are not always realistic and do not apply to a significant number of persons who present themselves for rape counseling. Helping agencies of all kinds are seeing an increase in serious mental and emotional distress among their clients, with more histories of severe physical and sexual abuse as well as emotional and medical neglect. Being raped can trigger memories of childhood sexual abuse, and the trauma of the current victimization can be significantly intensified by the unresolved trauma of the past (Dolan, 1991). At the same time, financial resources are diminishing for long-term mental health services, and we are seeing an increase in limits on number of sessions due to managed care, a move to brief therapy, and an overload on such broadly available services as are provided by rape crisis centers, community mental health centers, and college counseling centers (Gilbert, 1992).[7]

Because counselors in any setting can expect to frequently see victims for whom the presenting acquaintance rape is compounded by the victim's psychosocial history, the problem is how to provide appropriate services with limited resources to persons with complex needs. Such persons will typically include those with histories of chronic, unrelieved victimization, with symptoms that are consistent with a mental health diagnosis of a personality disorder (Herman, 1992).

The term *complex posttraumatic stress disorder* is recommended for two reasons. First, it is more accurate than posttraumatic stress disorder because it refers to a range of conditions and not to a single disorder. Second, the term helps to remove the stigma of a diagnostic label that implies a defect of character or personality and causes an abuse victim to be vulnerable to both a mistaken diagnosis and to misguided treatment (Herman, 1992). To assist the reader in identifying complex posttraumatic stress disorder, we are including a summary of symptoms recognized to be characteristic of persons with histories of prolonged victimization. This summary is based on the outline of symptoms defined in the proposed "new diagnosis" presented by Judith Herman (1992).

Summary of Symptoms for
Complex Posttraumatic Stress Disorder

1. *History.* There is a prolonged subjection to the total control of another person or persons. This may include being physically or sexually abused, being tortured, or being held hostage. It may also include being deprived of basic care and basic needs.
2. *Affect.* Mood disturbances are common including chronic depression or anxiety, suicidal preoccupation (gestures and attempts), self-injury (including self-mutilation), explosive anger or frozen affect, compulsive sexuality or sexual inhibition.
3. *States of Consciousness.* Dissociative states (splitting-off) are manifested on a continuum ranging from periodic memory loss and disorientation to, in some cases, multiple personalities. Intrusive thoughts or flashbacks (spontaneously reliving the trauma) may be present, the latter frequently being triggered by particular sights, sounds, and odors.
4. *Self-Perception.* The following symptoms may be noted: distorted self-concept associated with feelings of shame and self-blame, a sense of helplessness and powerlessness, a sense of being defiled or damaged, feeling different and disengaged from others associated with feeling special, unique, or nonhuman.

5. *Perceptions About the Perpetrator.* A preoccupation with the relationship to the perpetrator may be present including excessive attributions of power to the perpetrator (although the power of the perpetrator should not be completely discounted), idealization of the
   perpetrator, and seeing the relationship as special or supernatural.
   An acceptance of the perpetrator's way of thinking and believing
   may be evident.
6. *Relationships With Others.* The victim may be socially isolated and may
   display an inability to sustain close relationships and develop intimacy. A search for a rescuer may be noted alternating with a search
   for a persecutor (wanting to be protected/wanting to be punished).
   The following symptoms may also be noted in relationships: distrust
   or indiscriminate trust, a lack of boundaries or a "walled fortress,"
   and an inability to read social cues and make sound judgments about
   interpersonal relationships.
7. *Sense of Meaning.* The victim may demonstrate a sense of "free-falling"
   —namely, a feeling that nothing or no one is there, a feeling of empti-
   ness, a lack of faith and trust in the world and in other people, a sense
   of futurelessness and despair.

Knowing One's Limitations

The dilemma for many helping professionals is that although
they may wish to help everyone who seeks their services, they may
lack the expertise as well as the resources to provide interventions
for more serious and complicated needs, particularly when survivors of repeated abuse frequently become at risk to self-harm or
harm to others. The issue is not only *can* one provide services for
complex disorders but also *should* one provide such services, because
service provision under some circumstances presents risks not only
for the client but for the counselor as well (Gilbert, 1992). Persons
who have histories of repeated, unrelieved abuse are vulnerable to
suicide, self-mutilation, and other self-harming behaviors. Also,
they may become physically aggressive, sexually aggressive, or both
in their attempts to gain a sense of control of their pain. Such persons
are at risk with the inexperienced counselor who is not prepared to
respond appropriately and effectively to their needs. The counselor

is at risk of becoming a target of their aggressions, and/or to legal consequences for failure to treat in a professional and responsible manner, and/or failure to prevent harm.

The following recommendations are intended as guidelines for potential service providers to persons with symptoms of complex posttraumatic stress disorder as previously defined. These recommendations should be considered in the light of already existing agency policies.

1. A skillful assessment (by the counselor, supervisor, or consultant) should be available to any survivor who presents evidence of symptoms of complex posttraumatic stress disorder to determine the level of needs.

2. Referral options should be considered if these are warranted by the helper's or agency's limitations. It is important, however, to be aware of the limitations of certain other therapeutic approaches. Before making a referral, know the therapist or agency. Many therapists lack experience and training and many have antiquated, stereotypical, and (perhaps unconsciously) demeaning attitudes that are ultimately antitherapeutic. They may deny or diminish the victim's experience; they may distance from persons they perceive as weak or vulnerable. This can be true regardless of the gender of the counselor (Laidlaw et al., 1990). If there is a decision to provide services, after a thorough and comprehensive assessment and a review of the referral options, a commitment to a team approach with ongoing supervision for the counselor is advised.

Summary

The experiences of acquaintance rape victims differ from the experiences of other trauma victims because of the interpersonal and societal context of rape by a known perpetrator. The victim's inability to name the trauma a rape and her self-blame interfere with help seeking and prolong symptoms that seriously interfere with psychosocial well-being. Interventions must address the needs of both the recent and the nonrecent victim, including the need for cognitively restructuring beliefs about the world and reframing negative self-evaluation. Recovery is identified as the ability to recall the rape event without reliving it, a present and future orientation with connections to life tasks and other persons, a sense of self-worth and self-mastery, and the ability to integrate and resolve the rape in a meaningful way. The survivor with a history of repeated abuse may present symptoms of complex posttraumatic stress disorder and may require more intensive intervention than the counselor, the agency, or both can provide. In such cases, careful assessment, possible referral, or intervention with supervision and a team approach are advised. In all cases, the needs and the well-being of the survivor will be the primary considerations.

Notes

1. Helping professionals in both mental health and medical settings should be alert to the possibilities of undisclosed past sexual trauma and should be prepared to question clients when symptoms of sexual abuse trauma are present. For guidelines for interview, see Struckman-Johnson, 1991. This interview format is transferable to female clients.

2. For the relationship between sexual victimization, body image, and eating disorders, see Laidlaw and "Michaela," 1990.

3. The reader will note that this work and others cited in this chapter specifically address the needs of incest and child sexual abuse survivors. Incest and child sexual abuse literature, however, is transferable to the dynamics and recovery issues of acquaintance rape survivors.

4. Specific interventions that help to stabilize the traumatic crisis of talking about the sexual victimization and help the survivor to safely externalize painful memories are found in Chapters 2 through 10, pages 24-178. See also, Laidlaw et al., 1990, Chapters 6 through 12, pp. 83-271.

5. The author includes specific information for significant others throughout the book. See especially Chapters 1 through 8.

6. Readers who wish to develop psychoeducational group services for acquaintance rape survivors will find an excellent resource in Issori and Reubin, 1986.

7. The overextension of free and/or adjusted-fee mental health services is documented here for college counseling centers and generalized to community mental health and rape crisis centers, which often have waiting lists for services, except for emergencies.

Speak out! Acquaintance rape can survive only in silence.
—An acquaintance rape survivor

11 Preventing Acquaintance Rape

As we have seen in earlier chapters, acquaintance rape is a serious problem. Although we can help survivors in their recovery from this trauma, we must also consider how the problem can be prevented. This chapter will focus on ways acquaintance rape may be prevented. Prevention will be discussed at three different levels: (a) at the individual level of interpersonal relationships, (b) at the group level by focusing on educational efforts, and (c) at the societal level by creating social change.

Prevention at the Personal Level

Preventive efforts at the personal level focus on men assuming responsibility for their behavior in interpersonal relationships with women, and on women being aware of high-risk situations that may lead to acquaintance rape.

Males Assuming
Responsibility for Their Behavior

Commonly held myths about acquaintance rape, identified in an earlier chapter, frequently are used by males to excuse their sexually aggressive behavior. Preventive efforts with males must focus on their responsibility for sexual behavior, or conversely, on the fact that the use of rape-supportive myths represents an avoidance by men of taking responsibility for their sexual behavior.

Projecting the blame on the victim represents a myth commonly used by men to avoid responsibility for their actions. Rationalizations, such as the way an acquaintance was dressed, her actions or behaviors that led him on, or that the perpetrator was using drugs or alcohol and was not fully aware of his behavior, shifts the blame outside the male to his partner or to an external factor.

Education for preventing sexually aggressive behavior in males must expose these rationalizations as well as attack traditional stereotypical views held of women, for example, that "No" really doesn't mean "No." The eradication of such myths calls for educating men to engage in discussion with acquaintances and thereby to clarify with partners their intent regarding sexual activity rather than making incorrect assumptions that may lead to inappropriate behavior (see Box 11.1). Role playing is an effective method to use for teaching clarification of unclear or mixed messages.

An understanding of sexual arousal and the cognitive process in which a man should engage prior to acting on this physiological stimulus can serve as a tool in acquaintance rape prevention with men. The five-part model presented in Chapter 7 represents a step by step process the male must follow when experiencing sexual arousal (Hall & Hirschman, 1991). This model can be used to teach men to be aware of their thoughts, feelings, and behavior in interpersonal relationships with women, especially in situations involving sexual feelings. Such education should emphasize sexual arousal as a stimulus to *think* rather than as a stimulus to *act*.

Finally, preventive efforts must be directed toward helping men not only to respect their partner's wishes regarding whether or not to engage in sexual intimacy, but also to deal with their own feelings

BOX 11.1

Real Men Don't Rape

Real men accept the responsibility to not harm another person. It is never OK to force yourself on a woman, even if:

she teases you
dresses provocatively or leads you on
she says "No" and you think she means "Yes"
you've had sex before with her
you've paid for her dinner or given her expensive gifts
you think women enjoy being forced to have sex or want to be punished
the woman is under the influence of alcohol or drugs

- Rape is a crime of violence. It is motivated primarily by desire to control and dominate, rather than by sex. It is illegal.
- If you are getting a double message from a woman, speak up and clarify what she wants. If you find yourself in a situation with a woman who is unsure about having sex or is saying "No," back off. Suggest talking about it.
- Do not assume you know what your partner wants; check out your assumptions.
- Be sensitive to women who are unsure whether they want to have sex. If you put pressure on them, you may be forcing them.
- Do not assume you both want the same degree of intimacy. She may be interested in some sexual contact other than intercourse. There may be several kinds of sexual activity you might mutually agree to share.
- Stay in touch with your sexual desires. Ask yourself if you are really hearing what she wants. Do not let your desires control your actions.
- Communicate your sexual desires honestly and as early as possible.

- If you have *any* doubts about what your partner wants, STOP, ASK, CLARIFY.
- Your *desires* may be beyond your control, but your *actions* are within your control. Sexual excitement does not justify forced sex.
- Do not assume her desire for affection is the same as a desire for intercourse.
- Not having sex or not "scoring" does not mean you are not a "real man." It is OK not to "score."
- A woman who turns you down for sex is not necessarily rejecting you as a person; she is expressing her decision not to participate in a single act at that time.
- No one *asks* to be raped. No matter how a woman behaves, she does not deserve to have her body used in ways she does not want.
- "No" means *no*. If you do not accept a woman's "No," you might risk raping someone who you *thought* meant "Yes."
- Taking sexual advantage of a person who is mentally or physically incapable of giving consent (e.g., drunk) is rape. If a woman has had too much to drink and has passed out, or is not in control of herself, having sex with her is rape.
- The fact that you were intoxicated is not a legal defense to rape. You are responsible for your actions, whether you are sober or not.
- Be aware that a man's size and physical presence can be intimidating to a woman. Many victims report that the fear they felt based on the man's size and presence was the reason why they did not fight back or struggle.

SOURCE: Hughes and Sandler (1987). Copyright © Center for Women Policy Studies, 2000 P. Street, NW, Suite 508, Washington, DC 20036. Reprinted with permission.
NOTE: Men can be victims of rape and have the same rights to counseling and legal action as women do.

when a response of nonconsent occurs from their partner (see Box 11.2). Frequently, men regard nonconsent as rejection, a threat to their manhood, or as a challenge to press even harder for sexual intimacy. An excellent booklet, titled *Man-to-Man: When Your Partner Says "No,"* is available for purchase from the Safer Society Press (Shoreham Depot Road, RR1, Box 24-B, Orwell, VT 05760-9756,

BOX 11.2

Dating Rights Statements

1. I have the right to refuse a date without feeling guilty.
2. I have the right to ask for a date without being crushed if the answer is "No."
3. I have the right to choose to go somewhere alone without having to pair up with someone.
4. I have the right not to act "macho" or seductive.
5. I have the right to say "No" to physical closeness.
6. I have the right to say, "I want to know you better before I become involved or before we have sex."
7. I have the right to say, "I don't want to be in this relationship any longer."
8. I have the right to equal relationships.
9. I have the right not to be abused physically, sexually, or emotionally.
10. I have the right to change my life goals whenever I want.
11. I have the right to have friends, including those of the opposite sex.
12. I have the right to express my feelings.
13. I have the right to set limits, to say "No" or "Yes," and to change my mind if I so choose, without permission from anyone else.
14. I have the right to stop doing something, even in the middle of it.
15. I have the right to have my morals, values, and beliefs respected.
16. I have the right to say "I love you" without having sex.
17. I have the right to be ME, even if it is different from the "norm," or from what you want me to be.
18. I have the right to say "I don't want to please you at this time, or do that."
19. I have the right to talk with others about my relationships.
20. I have the right to be as open or as closed as I feel comfortable.

SOURCE: From *Man-to-Man: When Your Partner Says "No,"* by Scott A. Johnson (1992). Orwell, VT: Safer Society Press. Reprinted with permission.

802-897-7541). The booklet, although written as a guide for men, discusses the pressures men experience to engage in sexual intimacy as an expected but inappropriate norm, and the implications of their behavior.

Situations That May Lead to Rape

Education at the individual level in acquaintance rape prevention with women may focus on helping them develop an awareness of situations that might lead to sexually aggressive behavior. Although women cannot always avoid rape by an acquaintance, the following are suggestions addressed to women that they can follow in minimizing their chances of being raped (Hughes & Sandler, 1987).

1. Examine your feelings about sex. Many women have been socialized to believe that sex means that they will be swept away with the emotion of the moment or that they can "make out" and then decide whether to say "Yes" or "No" to sex later. The problem with this kind of thinking is that it gives too much control to the other person.

2. Set sexual limits. It is your body, and no one has the right to force you to do anything you do not want to do. If you do not want someone to touch you or kiss you, for example, you can say, "Take your hands off me," or "Don't touch me," or "If you don't respect my wishes right now, I'm leaving." Stopping sexual activity does not mean that anything is wrong with you, or that you are not a "real" woman.

3. Decide early if you would like to have sex. The sooner you communicate firmly and clearly your sexual intentions the easier it will be for your partner to hear and accept your decision.

4. Do not give mixed messages—be clear. Say "Yes" when you mean "Yes" and say "No" when you mean "No." (The ability to be assertive can be developed by training and practice.)

5. Be alert to other unconscious messages you may be giving. Men may interpret your behavior differently from what you intended. Often women and men send strong nonverbal signs of willingness to enter a sexual relationship and unintentional signals that might conflict with their words, and thereby contribute to sexual assault. Be aware of signals you send with your posture, clothing, tone of voice, gestures, and eye contact.

6. Be forceful and firm. Do not worry about not being "polite." Often, men interpret passivity as permission; they may ignore or misunderstand "nice" or "polite" approaches. Say something like "Stop this. I'm not enjoying it," or "Your behavior is not encouraging an open relationship between us." If a woman ignores sexual activity she does not like, a man is likely to interpret that as tacit approval for him to continue. Men are not mind readers.

7. Be independent and aware of your dates. Do not be totally passive. Do have opinions on where to go. Do think about appropriate places to meet (not necessarily at your apartment or his), and, if possible, pay your own way or suggest activities that do not cost any money.

8. Do not do anything you do not want to just to avoid a scene or unpleasantness. Women have been socialized to be polite. In an effort to be nice, they may be reluctant to yell or run away or escape being attacked. Do not be raped because you were too polite to get out of a dangerous situation. If you are worried about hurting his feelings, remember, he is ignoring *your* feelings. Be aware of how stereotypes about women may affect your behavior. Accepting beliefs that "women shouldn't express themselves strongly" or that "anger is unfeminine" make women more vulnerable.

9. Be aware of specific situations in which you do not feel relaxed and in charge. Unwillingness to acknowledge a situation as potentially dangerous and a reluctance to appear oversensitive often hold women back from responding in the interest of their own safety. For example, avoid attending or staying late at parties where men greatly outnumber women. Do not be afraid to leave early just because it might seem rude. Situations where there are few women around can quickly get out of hand.

10. If things start to get out of hand, be loud in protesting, leave, go for help. Do not wait for someone else to rescue you or for things to get better. If it feels uncomfortable, leave quickly.

11. Trust your gut-level feelings. If you feel you are being pressured, you probably are, and you need to respond. If a situation feels bad, or you start to get nervous about the way your date is acting, confront the person immediately or leave the situation as quickly as possible.

12. Be aware that alcohol and drugs are often related to acquaintance rape. They compromise your ability (and that of your date) to make responsible decisions. If you choose to drink alcohol, drink responsibly. Be able to get yourself home and do not rely on others to "take care" of you.

13. Avoid falling for such lines as "You would if you loved me." If he loves you, he will respect your feelings and will wait until you are ready.

14. If you are unsure of a new acquaintance, go on a group or double date. If this is not possible, meet him in a public place and have your own transportation home.

15. Have your own transportation, if possible, or taxi fare. At least for the first few dates, this establishes your independence and makes you appear to be a less vulnerable target.

16. Avoid secluded places where you are in a vulnerable position. This is especially critical at the beginning of a relationship. Establish a pattern of going where there are other people, where you feel comfortable and safe. This will give you a chance to get to know your date better and decide if you wish to continue dating him.

17. Be careful when you invite someone to your home or you are invited to his home. These are the most likely places where acquaintance rapes occur.

18. Examine your attitudes about money and power. If he pays for the date, does that influence your ability to say "No?" If so, then pay your own way or suggest dates that do not involve money.

19. Think about the pros and cons of dating much older men. Although they may be sophisticated and have the money to treat you well, they may also be more sexually experienced and may therefore expect more sooner.

20. Socialize with people who share your values. If you go out with people who are more sexually permissive than you are, you may be perceived as sharing those values.[1]

Prevention at the Community Level

Preventive Efforts in Educational Settings

Group educational efforts toward preventing acquaintance rape generally occur in high school, college, or university settings. Such preventive efforts may be already initiated in junior high or even earlier when students are beginning to date. Research shows that educational efforts aimed at preventing acquaintance rape must start at a very early age because many early teens have considerable misinformation about rape. A study involving young teenagers found that they were relatively unaware that individuals who rape may appear very normal and may be an acquaintance of the victim (Hall, 1987). Educational efforts aimed at preventing acquaintance rape should continue through college when students may be at greatest risk for committing sexual assault or being victimized.

Two student-related target groups are suggested for preventive education. The first includes young adults meeting together in groups, such as students attending freshman orientation or participating in campus organizations; residents in dormitories, fraternity and sorority houses; and members of high school and collegiate athletic teams.

Group educational efforts with students may be built around the following goals:

1. To develop an awareness of the problem of acquaintance rape and that each person has the potential to be a victim or perpetrator
2. To sensitize students to the role alcohol and drugs play in creating a setting where acquaintance rape may more likely occur
3. To inform students that their safety and sexual well-being are their personal responsibility and these goals are attained when they communicate effectively and assertively in their interpersonal relationships with members of the opposite sex
4. To inform students of where to go and what they should do if they are sexually victimized by an acquaintance (Miller, 1988)

The second group to which preventive education on acquaintance rape should be directed is personnel working with students. These include student affairs personnel, high school and college counselors, residence advisors, staff in student health clinics, and supportive personnel to athletic teams. Preventive educational efforts directed to these target groups should not only include an awareness of the nature and scope of the problem of acquaintance rape, but also specialized training in the identification, assessment, and treatment of the problem, including a workable knowledge of how and where to make a referral of victims.

Although research on the status of educational efforts on college campuses reflects that most such programs are conducted by college or university counseling centers, this presents the view that sexual abuse in the dating relationship is a mental health issue rather than a university-wide issue of concern to administration, faculty, staff, and students. The fact that school counseling centers primarily assume responsibility for such educational efforts is not necessarily negative, however, it has implications for the nature of the program and the extent to which the university views the problem as one potentially affecting all students. Also, a counseling center does not have the authority to create or enforce school policy on this issue (Bogal-Allbritten & Allbritten, 1990).

Educational programs for acquaintance rape prevention will differ based on the gender of the participants, the size of the group, and the setting. For example, educational programs directed to international students in a college or university setting should include information on cultural attitudes toward interpersonal relationships between the sexes that might not be included in a program for students in a fraternity, sorority, or dormitory setting.

Numerous resources are available when designing a program on acquaintance rape prevention for groups. Rape crisis centers located in most communities throughout the United States can serve as a valuable resource in assisting you in the design and implementation of group educational programs focusing on acquaintance rape prevention.

In the Appendix you will find two examples of acquaintance rape education programs. The first program titled, "Sex: A Decision for Two," was developed by Planned Parenthood of Greater Northern New Jersey and is used on college campuses. This program examines the concept of "safer sex" and broadens the definition of this term to include being safe from unwanted or nonconsenual sexual activity.

The second program in the Appendix was developed by Diana Pace and Dr. John Zaugra of Grand Valley State University, Allendale, Michigan. This program, although developed for college students, can be adapted for use with other age groups. Both examples are presented as programs that have effectively been used in educating individuals at risk for being victims or perpetrators of acquaintance rape. The programs may be modified to suit your individual needs.

Printed materials can effectively be used in preventive educational efforts. An excellent pamphlet on acquaintance rape may be purchased from the American College Health Association (P.O. Box 28937, Baltimore, MD 21240-8937, 410-859-1500). This pamphlet can be used in educational programs for high school and college students. It provides information on how the stage is often set for acquaintance rape, steps individuals can take to avoid the problem, how to help a friend who has been raped by an acquaintance, and what to expect in the process of recovering from an acquaintance rape.

Another tool that can be used in creative programming with groups is a questionnaire titled, "Attitudes Toward Forcible Date Rape Scale" (see Box 11.3). This instrument assesses attitudes toward date rape. It can be given to groups of people and their responses can serve as the basis for discussion of commonly held myths regarding date rape that underlie many of the questions. In discussing responses to each question, the group leader can present correct information on the subject or show an educational film or video on acquaintance rape.

An array of films and videos are available for creatively designing acquaintance rape prevention programs. Following are selected films/videos on acquaintance rape and the source for where they can be rented or purchased.

Date Rape: It Happened to Me

This video, directed to students at junior high and high school levels, aims at sensitizing teenagers to the emotional, psychological, and legal ramifications of an act of sexual violence. A dramatized incident of date rape is combined with narration by teenage hosts, first-person accounts of date rape victims, and observations by law officers and adult counselors. The video covers prevention, treatment, and recovery aspects of date rape. (30 minutes)

Available from Pyramid Film and Video, P.O. Box 1048, Santa Monica, CA 90406-1048, (800) 421-2304.

BOX 11.3

Attitudes Toward
Forcible Date Rape Scale

A male and female college student go out on a date. Afterward, they go to his apartment and sit in front of the fireplace for a while and sip a glass of wine. He kisses her and, even though she resists his advances, uses his superior strength to force her to have sexual intercourse.

1. Would you call this rape?
   A. Definitely
   B. Probably
   C. Not sure
   D. Probably not
   E. Definitely not
2. If rape did occur, where does the fault *mainly* lie?
   A. The male
   B. The situation—the apartment and alcohol was an avoidable risk and/or temptation
   C. Society—for the way it socializes males and reinforces their dominant and assertive behavior
   D. The female

For each of the conditions in 1-9 below, indicate how acceptable you consider the male's behavior in the above example by circling one of the following responses:

   A. Definitely acceptable
   B. Moderately acceptable
   C. Mildly acceptable
   D. Not sure
   E. Mildly unacceptable
   F. Moderately unacceptable
   G. Definitely unacceptable

1. If he had spent a lot of money on her.

   A   B   C   D   E   F   G

2. If she had gotten him sexually excited.

   A   B   C   D   E   F   G

3. If she left him touch her breasts.

   A   B   C   D   E   F   G

4. If they had dated each other for a long time.

   A   B   C   D   E   F   G

5. If she was drunk.

   A   B   C   D   E   F   G

6. If she was going to have intercourse with him and then changed her mind.

   A   B   C   D   E   F   G

7. If she had intercourse with other males.

   A   B   C   D   E   F   G

8. If she led him on.

   A   B   C   D   E   F   G

9. If he was so sexually excited he couldn't stop.

   A   B   C   D   E   F   G

SOURCE: Fischer, G. J. (1986). College student attitudes toward forcible date rape: I. Cognitive predictors. *Archives of Sexual Behavior, 15,* 457-466. Reprinted with permission.

Date Rape on the College Campus

The date rape problem is the focus of this specially adapted Phil Donahue program that shows how women at Brown University are fighting back against date rape. A group called "Stop Campus Rape" is encouraging female students to write the names of their attackers on the school's bathroom walls. The issue has divided the student body. Male students fear they will be falsely accused; female students feel that unless they take a stand, they will continue to be victimized. (28 minutes)

Available from Films for the Humanities & Sciences, P.O. Box 2053, Princeton, NJ 08543-2053, (800) 257-5126.

When Date Becomes Rape

This video contains factual information for combating date rape. It includes interviews with experts in the fields of sociology, anthropology, psychology, and rape counseling. The video discusses the societal causes for rape and presents valuable information on prevention and treatment. (20 minutes)

Available from Nimco, 117 Highway 815, P.O. Box 9, Calhoun, KY 42327, (800) 962-6662.

Acquaintance Rape

This CINE Golden Eagle award-winning documentary profiles the case of a young man, a former football hero and honor roll student, sentenced at age 22 to life in prison for the murder of a coworker. In examining the pervasiveness of violence between people who know each other, this program provides information on the relationship between stress and violence, the impact of television and movie violence, and the consequences of society's sanction of violence as an acceptable form of conflict resolution. (16 minutes)

Available from Coronet/MTI Film & Video, 4350 Equity Drive, Columbus, OH 43228, (800) 321-3106.

Against Her Will: Rape on Campus

Hosted by actress Kelly McGillis, this candid documentary explores the "whys" of acquaintance rape and examines what parents can do to better prepare their children for new freedoms that come hand-in-hand with contemporary campus life. Designed to raise student awareness in how they can protect themselves and each other, this video also details educational and security measures colleges and universities can take to stop the epidemic of acquaintance rape. Candid interviews with female rape victims, young male students, security personnel, and counselors help to underscore the growing horror of rape on college campuses. (46 minutes)

Available from Coronet/MTI Film & Video, 4350 Equity Drive, Columbus, OH 43228, (800) 321-3106.

Not Only Strangers

Realistically portraying Sarah's emotional shock, revulsion, guilt, and ultimate anger after being raped by a classmate, this video gives the audience a comprehensive understanding of the painful but necessary process of filing criminal charges. The video contains explicit language and is not recommended for showing to young children. (23 minutes)

Available from Coronet/MTI Film & Video, 4350 Equity Drive, Columbus, OH 43228, (800) 321-3106.

Rape Prevention: Trust Your Instincts

Although no rape victim could have accurately predicted when or where she would be sexually assaulted, in the aftermath many women have recognized suppressing a feeling of danger shortly before the attack. If heeded, that feeling could have possibly averted the assault. In teaching women to raise their level of awareness to surroundings, and to project the kind of nonverbal assertiveness that makes them an "unattractive" mark, this program instills an effective nonviolent approach to rape prevention. Dramatizations illustrate situations where women should trust their instincts, and also presents a chance to practice nonviolent response options that can dramatically reduce panic and fear during the initial stages of a physical confrontation. (18 minutes)

Available from Coronet/MTI Film & Video, 4350 Equity Drive, Columbus, OH 43228, (800) 321-3106.

Preventive Efforts in Communities

"Take Back the Night" and the Clothesline Project are advocacy efforts that are initiated by local communities to promote public education and awareness about the problem of sexual assault and to provide a healing and empowering experience for survivors.

"Take Back the Night" rallies and marches first began in England as a protest against the fear that women encountered walking the streets at night. The first "Take Back the Night" rally and march held in the United States occurred in San Francisco in 1978. Since that time, "Take Back the Night" events have spread throughout the nation, growing steadily in their numbers and strength. These rallies and marches take a variety of forms. Some feature workshops, music, and films whereas others present speakers addressing the issue of interpersonal violence or survivors telling their stories. Although they may take a variety of forms, the unifying purpose of "Take Back the Night" is the self-empowerment of persons who have experienced victimization by sexual assault or domestic violence. A "Take Back the Night" organizing manual is available from: United Council, 122 State Street, Suite 500, Madison, WI 53703, (608) 263-3422.

The Clothesline Project is a visual display that bears witness to violence against women. During the public display, a clothesline is hung with shirts. Each shirt is decorated by the survivor herself or by someone who cares about her to represent her particular experience. A color code identifies the type of victimization. For further information contact: The Clothesline Project, Box 727, East Dennis, MA 02641, (508) 385-7004.

Prevention at the Societal Level

Although acquaintance rape is perceived as a personal problem and its impact is most severely felt by each individual survivor, in reality this social problem is a societal problem. Social problems occur when the institutions and mechanisms society creates to carry out its basic functions do not exist, operate ineffectively, or serve to oppress and exploit society's least powerful members (*A Generalist Perspective*, 1992).

Acquaintance rape reflects the failure of society to achieve several of its primary functions—namely, to provide opportunities for growth, development, and life enhancement and to protect its members. Societal failure to fulfill its function in these areas occurs along the dimension of gender. The feminist theory of rape, discussed earlier, emphasizes the disparity of social, political, and economic power that exists between the sexes resulting from long and deep-seated social traditions (Ellis, 1989).

A societal approach to acquaintance rape prevention calls for a correction of societal institutions and the mechanisms for carrying out basic societal functions that fail to provide equal treatment to all members of society regardless of gender. Any breakdown that occurs in society providing its basic functions to all members, regardless of gender, requires the development and implementation of strategies for creating sociopolitical change. This is the responsibility of and a task for all societal members. Again, we come back to the individual members of society. The confrontation of acquaintance rape supportive myths and traditional stereotypical views of male/female relationships must occur at all societal levels beginning in the context of the family and continuing through to the nation that implements policies and laws that affect its citizens.

Summary

The prevention of acquaintance rape, a serious problem in American society, must occur at the personal, group, and societal level. At the personal level, males must assume responsibility for sexually aggressive behavior against females rather than hiding behind acquaintance rape myths. At the group level, many resources in the form of speakers available from rape crisis centers, as well as pamphlets, films, and videos, can be used with student groups from junior high schools through colleges and universities. Acquaintance rape prevention must also occur at the societal level with the formation of public policy that provides opportunities for development, life enhancement, and protection regardless of gender.

Note

1. The 20-item list is from Hughes and Sandler (1987). Copyright © Center for Women Policy Studies, 2000 P Street, NW, Suite 508, Washington, DC 20036. Reprinted with permission.

APPENDIX A

The Research Questionnaire

Rape crisis centers in the United States were sent a letter explaining the research project on acquaintance rape and a copy of the research questionnaire that is duplicated on the following pages. Rape crisis centers were asked to return a postcard requesting additional copies of the questionnaire for distribution to clients who had been raped by an acquaintance. Space was provided in the questionnaire following the open-ended questions that is not shown in the duplication of the instrument below.

Cover Letter

Dear Respondent,

Thank you for your willingness to participate in this research on acquaintance rape. Although this has been a common problem in our society for decades, an awareness of this problem is just beginning.

A lack of information exists on the problem of acquaintance rape. The purpose of this research is to gather information from survivors and to compile this information into a book which will increase the public's awareness of this serious social problem so that it can be prevented and the survivors treated.

You can help us by completing the following questionnaire. We want to assure you any information from the questionnaires will be dealt with anonymously and all identifying data will be removed or changed. Do not return this questionnaire if you are under 18 years of age. Thank you for your willingness to complete the questionnaire. You will find an addressed postage paid envelope attached for your convenience in returning the questionnaire to us.

Sincerely,

Vernon R. Wiehe, Ph.D.
Lorna Nichols, B.G.S.

College of Social Work
University of Kentucky
661 Patterson Office Tower
Lexington, KY 40506-0027
(606) 257-6657

Definitions

Following are some definitions for terms that will be used in the questionnaire. Please read these definitions *before* proceeding to answer the Questionnaire.

Acquaintance rape: any sexual activity that one experiences, without giving consent, with someone that the individual *dates* or *knows*. This includes fondling, oral sex, anal sex, intercourse, or other sexual activity. This questionnaire is *not* for survivors of stranger rape; namely, rape by a person *unknown* to the survivor.

Perpetrator: the person who initiates sexual activity, *without* the consent of their partner. This may include someone you have dated or known, such as a classmate, fellow employee, resident in your apartment building, therapist, physician, spouse, relative, and so forth.

Survivor: the person who has been raped. Often the word "victim" is used to describe a person who has been raped; however, we prefer to use the word "survivor" because it is a more empowering or positive expression.

Note: If you have been acquaintance raped more than once, please respond to the questionnaire on the basis of the most recent rape. If you wish to share any information about other rapes, please do so on a separate sheet of paper.

Questionnaire

1. Age: _____
2. Race: _____ Caucasian _____ African American _____ Other _____
3. Your Education. Please check highest level of school you have completed:
   _____ less than 10th grade
   _____ partial high school (10th grade)
   _____ high school graduate or GED
   _____ partial college (at least 1 year or specialized training
   _____ college or university graduate
   _____ graduate or professional education (graduate degree)

4. At the time of the acquaintance rape, were you: (Check all that apply)

_____ an undergraduate student

_____ a graduate student

_____ working part-time

_____ working full-time

_____ a high school student

_____ other (please specify) _____

5. What were the approximate ages of you and the perpetrator at the time of the rape?

_____ you   _____ perpetrator

6. To your knowledge, were you abused as a child by a family member:

_____ emotionally

_____ physically

_____ sexually

_____ not at all

7. Have you received counseling for acquaintance rape?

_____ yes   _____ no

If yes, please check one or more of the following:

_____ clergy

_____ private therapist

_____ community mental health center

_____ rape crisis center

other (please specify) _____

8. Were you raped by your spouse? (Marital rape *is* included in our definition of acquaintance rape.)

_____ yes   _____ no

If no, proceed to Question 9.

If yes, answer a, b, c, d below.

(a) Have you been raped more than once by your spouse?

_____ yes   _____ no

If yes, approximately how many times?

(b) How long did you know your spouse before the rape occurred, or the first rape, if more than one?

(c) How long ago did the rape, or most recent rape, occur?

(d) Were you living with your spouse at the time of the rape, or most recent rape?

_____ yes   _____ no

(NOW PLEASE SKIP TO QUESTION 16)

9. How did you meet the perpetrator, and/or how are you related to the perpetrator? (Please specify.)

10. How many perpetrators were there?

11. How long did you know the perpetrator before the rape occurred?

12. How well did you know the perpetrator?

(Circle the appropriate number)

1	2	3	4	5
knew very well		knew somewhat		knew only distantly/ just met

13. Did the rape occur with a man you were dating?

_____ yes   _____ no

If yes, how many times had you dated before the rape occurred?

14. Did the rape occur with a man you were engaged to?

_____ yes   _____ no

If yes, how many times had you dated before the rape occurred?

15. (a) How long ago did the rape occur?

(b) Where did the rape occur?
(car, your apartment, his apartment, dorm room, etc.)

16. Sometimes women who are raped can look back and recognize behavior by the perpetrator that made them uncomfortable before the rape occurred. As you look back, if there were any behaviors of the perpetrator that made you feel uncomfortable before the rape occurred, please share what the behaviors were.

17. At the time of the rape, was the perpetrator using alcohol or drugs? If so, how much?

18. Research indicates that a woman who is raped while using drugs or alcohol often experiences more *self-blame*, is *less likely to report the rape*, and is *treated differently* by others. In your situation, were you using drugs or alcohol? If so, please share how it has affected the areas underlined above.

19. Often women have consented to sexual activity with the perpetrator before the rape. As a result, they may experience more self-blame. If there had been sexual activity with the perpetrator before the rape, please share how this has affected you.

20. If you did consent to any sexual activities before the rape, would you share which of the below were involved?

_____ kissing

_____ fondling

_____ intercourse

21. Sometimes women blame themselves for not being able to get away from the perpetrator, or somehow preventing the rape. Please share how this issue has affected you.

22. If force was used by the perpetrator, what types of force were used? (Check all that apply)

_____ verbal persuasion

_____ verbal threats

_____ physical intimidation

_____ drugged with alcohol or other drugs

_____ some physical roughness (slap or push)

_____ extreme physical roughness (beat, choke)

_____ display weapon

_____ injury with weapon

_____ other (please specify) _____

Please comment on any of the above.

23. What sexual violations were you forced into? (Check all that apply)

_____ fondling him   _____ him fondling you

_____ oral sex on him   _____ oral sex on you

_____ intercourse

_____ anal sex

_____ other activity (please specify) _____

Please comment on any of the above.

24. Please address anything about your experience that you would like us to know to educate the public about acquaintance rape.

25. (a) If you are unmarried, how do you feel the rape you experienced affects your dating patterns now? Please address how *trust* and *intimacy* specifically have been affected.

(b) If you are married, how has the rape(s) affected your marriage? Please address how *trust* and *intimacy* specifically have been affected.

26. Based on our definition, had you ever heard of "acquaintance rape" before it happened to you?

_____ yes   _____ no

27. Did you define your experience as rape at first? Please relate why or why not?

28. If you did not define it as rape at first, when did you define it as rape?

29. Did you report the rape to authorities? Please relate why you did or did not report it.

If you *did* report it, to whom did you report it, and what was your experience?

30. Did you seek medical assistance? If so, please relate your experience.

31. Did you prosecute the perpetrator? If so, please describe your experience, and especially what the outcome was.

32. Have you told anyone about the rape? If so, please share what their reactions were, and what their relationship is to you.

33. What one suggestion do you have for eliminating acquaintance rape in America?

Closing Comments

We recognize that completing this questionnaire may bring up unpleasant thoughts and feelings. If this has happened to you, and you feel that you need to talk to someone, please check your local directory for a rape crisis center or other counselor nearest to you.

THANK YOU FOR PARTICIPATING IN THIS RESEARCH!

Sex: A Decision for Two

Objectives

1. Participants will expand the concept of "safer sex" to include being safe from unwanted sexual activity.

2. Participants will recognize that a person's sexual safety is at risk whenever a couple is not communicating honestly and clearly about what is happening between them.

3. Participants will examine how traditional sex role expectations may program girls to be victims and boys to be offenders.

4. Participants will identify incidents of miscommunication and recommend behavior changes.

Rationale

During the past few years, "safer sex" has become equated with AIDS prevention and, to a lesser degree, with prevention of other sexually transmitted diseases. But a truly safe encounter must be free from fear of unwanted pregnancy and from coercion or pressure, as well as from disease. Yet, recent studies confirm that the sexual expectations of both males and females lead many to believe that force to achieve intercourse is acceptable and in fact expected in a variety of dating situations. This lesson seeks to provoke discussion about the assumptions and miscommunications that lead to the prevalence of "date rape." It provides strategies for preventing this all-too-common form of unsafe sex.

Materials

Worksheets: Sex: A Decision for Two Scenario
              The Analysis

Procedure

1. Tell participants you will read a series of sentence stems and they are to write the *first response* that comes to their mind for each. Encourage them *not* to think, but to record their "gut" reaction. As you read each sentence stem, write it on the blackboard:

    a. Sex is safer when . . .
    b. Boys have sex because . . .
    c. Girls have sex because . . .
    d. Sex is dangerous when . . .
    e. When girls say "no" they mean . . .
    f. When boys say "no" they mean . . .

2. Ask for three or four volunteers to read their responses to each item.

    Discussion Questions:

    a. Are the "gut" responses to the first sentence stem adequate for describing "safe sex" or do you want to add other characteristics that are necessary before you would consider an encounter to be "safe?"

b. Note that this lesson will examine the idea that when sex is forced, it is unsafe sex. A study in *Nobody Told Me It Was Rape* by Caren Adams and Jennifer Fay (1984) reports that 39% of teen males and 12% of teen females think it is okay for a boy to hold a girl down and force her to have sexual intercourse if he spends a lot of money on her; 39% of the males and 18% of the females think this is okay if she is stoned or drunk; and 51% of the males and 42% of the females think force is okay if she gets him sexually excited. Although all of the above describe rape, only 34% of the teens said that force was unacceptable in any of these circumstances. Ask, do attitudes about why boys/men have sex reveal anything about why "date rape" is so common today?

c. What can be done about the fact that some men believe that women do not mean "no" when they say "no?"

3. Distribute Worksheet: SEX: A DECISION FOR TWO—THE SCENARIO. You may read it yourself, or get two participants to read it as the group reads along.

4. Divide participants into small groups of 4 or 5 each. Distribute THE ANALYSIS and have groups complete it.

5. Ask participants to return to the whole group. Discuss THE ANALYSIS briefly, then ask the girls/women to quickly write all the ways they can help prevent "date rape" and ask the boys/men to write all the ways they can help prevent "date rape."

6. List the BRAINSTORMING from each group on the board.

Discussion Questions:

a. Do you think that understanding how "date rape" happens will help prevent it? Why or why not?

b. What skills would girls/women need to assert themselves in sexual situations?

c. What skills would boys/men need to be more aware of their partner's real feelings?

7. If there is time, distribute small file cards and ask each participant to write one thought and one feeling they have at the end of this lesson/ workshop. They should *not* put their names on the card.

Collect the cards, shuffle, redistribute and have each person read the card they now have. (This activity provides good closure and may set the direction for your next lesson/workshop.)

Worksheet:
SEX: A DECISION FOR TWO—THE SCENARIO

8:00 p.m.

"Hurry up," urged Yvonne. "I thought you said Willie would meet us downstairs at 8:00 p.m." Jill, Yvonne's roommate replied, "Yeah, I know. Listen, I forgot to mention—but that guy you know from English is gonna come with us. You remember, he's a good friend of Willie's." Yvonne felt nervous suddenly. "You mean John? You know I think he's really cute. What do I say?" Jill answered, "Just act natural." Yvonne nodded, thinking the party was going to be really good with John there.

8:15 p.m.

At the party, John was very attentive to Yvonne. She was thrilled. They started to dance. Yvonne knew she was a terrific dancer and she loved to dance, especially with such a cute guy as John. They spent about an hour together, alternating between talking and dancing. Yvonne had a few beers. She could feel her body get looser from the alcohol making her dancing, she felt, even better.

10:30 p.m.

A slow song came on and John immediately pulled Yvonne close. Yvonne did not feel entirely comfortable dancing in this way but did not say anything. Instead, she put her hands on his chest in an attempt to keep their bodies from pressing too close. John was really enjoying himself. He had noticed Yvonne in English and thought she was attractive. He couldn't believe his luck. He felt he was acting so smooth and charming. He could sense she was responding to it. He decided to kiss Yvonne.

Yvonne was surprised at John's kiss. She was attracted to him, yet felt uncomfortable that he was kissing her in public. She didn't want him to think that she didn't like him so she just tilted her head down to end the kiss. John thought to himself, she really likes me. She is snuggling in after that kiss.

11:30 p.m.

The dance floor became packed again as the music got fast. Yvonne felt slightly dizzy from the beer and wanted to get some air. John was distressed at the mood change. He felt very turned on and wanted to be alone with

Yvonne. He said to her, "Want to go outside for some air? It's pretty stuffy in here." Yvonne looked around for Jill but didn't see her. She said to John, "OK, but just for a little while." She felt very nervous about being with him alone, but felt silly feeling that way.

11:40 p.m.

Once outside, John immediately put his arm around Yvonne and began kissing her, thinking how much she wanted to be kissed because she had been dancing so sexy all evening. Yvonne, still unsure about what she wanted, pulled away and began talking about how good her freshman year had been so far. John thought she was quite drunk and was very talkative when drunk. So he continued to kiss her. Yvonne again pulled away and stood up saying, "I think I should get going. Let's find Jill."

12:00 midnight

John followed Yvonne inside to the party. They had found that Jill had just left with Willie. John offered to walk Yvonne to her dorm thinking he could spend some more time with her alone. Not wanting to walk alone, Yvonne agreed.

12:30 a.m.

Arriving at Yvonne's dark suite, John asked, "Aren't your roommates home?" Yvonne told him they were away. John thought to himself Yvonne wants to be alone with me too. That's why she brought me back here. John said to Yvonne, "Let's go inside then. We don't have to say goodnight out here." Yvonne hesitated. She told John that she was very tired and wanted to go to sleep. John said, "I won't stay long," and took her key from her hand and opened the door. When Yvonne stood in the hall and said goodnight, John laughed. John walked past her into the living room saying, "Come sit for awhile." He motioned to the space next to him on the couch.

Yvonne sat down, still buzzed from the beer, and began to explain once again that she was tired and John should stay only for a few minutes. John, thinking of how sexy Yvonne was, moved over and began to kiss her. He pushed her down onto the couch and began to unbutton her shirt. Yvonne did not respond to his kisses and pushed him away muttering, "No, stop." John ignored her, continuing to undress both of them thinking she really wanted it.

Yvonne stopped saying, "No" and began to cry when John began to have intercourse with her.

Worksheet: SEX: A DECISION FOR TWO—
THE ANALYSIS

1. Identify three times during the scenario when John did not respect Yvonne's feelings.

   a. _____

   b. _____

   c. _____

2. Identify three times during the scenario when Yvonne made herself more vulnerable.

   a. _____

   b. _____

   c. _____

3. If John were sensitive to his partner, what signals would have told him that Yvonne did not want to continue?

   a. _____

   b. _____

   c. _____

4. If Yvonne had been assertive, what three things could she have said to make her real feelings clear to John?

   a. _____

   b. _____

   c. _____

5. Date rape often proceeds through three stages. Identify behaviors in THE SCENARIO at each stage:

   a. Someone (usually the male) enters another's "personal space" in a public place (kissing, hand on breast or thigh, etc.).

   _____

   b. The partner does not assertively stop this intrusion and the aggressor assumes it's OK.

   _____

   c. The aggressor gets the couple to a secluded place where the rape occurs.

   _____

SOURCE: Brick, P., et al. (1989). *Teaching Safer Sex*. (Planned Parenthood of Greater Northern New Jersey, 575 Main Street, Hacksensack, NJ 07601). Reprinted with permission.

A Date Rape Workshop

Diana Pace, PhD
John Zaugra, EdD
Counseling Center
Grand Valley State University
Allendale, MI 49401-9403

History: The date rape workshop at Grand Valley State University evolved out of increased awareness among the Counseling Center staff regarding the prevalence of date rape and an increase in the number of students who presented date rape as a clinical concern in counseling.

In an effort to increase staff's skills regarding date rape, the Center sent a male staff member to a date rape training workshop by Andrea Parrot in 1985. A male was intentionally chosen to attend because female staff members were already somewhat aware of the dynamics of date rape and were feeling some degree of outrage about it. The need was felt for both males and females to develop sensitivity to this social problem and ways to intervene.

Workshop Schedule: The workshop requires approximately two and one-half hours. However, this time period can be shortened by not showing a video and eliminating one of the exercises. The number in parentheses indicates minutes devoted to that program item.

(5) Introduction of facilitators and brief overview of the workshop. (Workshops are conducted by a male and female facilitator.)

(20) Administration of *Date Quiz* and *The Anatomy of a Date Rape.* (See end of this section for these items.) Discussion of responses and brief presentation of general information on date rape.

(20) Administration of *Sexual Assertiveness Questionnaire* and discussion of responses. (See end of this section for this item.)

(35) Video. (See videos reviewed in Chapter 11—"Preventing Acquaintance Rape.")

(10) Group discussion of video.

(45) *Fishbowl Exercise.*

(5) Distribution of materials on date rape prevention. (See suggested pamphlets in Chapter 11 or materials may be acquired from your local rape crisis center.)

(5) Completion of the *Date-Rape Workshop Evaluation Form.*

Date Quiz

1. In what percentage of the cases are men sexual assault victims?

   0%   10%   20%   30%   40%

2. Rape can occur in a relationship characterized by trust and respect.

   Yes   No

3. Date rape is prevalent among all socioeconomic, educational, and occupational classes.

   Yes   No

4. If a woman goes to a man's place of residence, it means she is willing to have sex.

   Yes   No

5. Miscommunication about sex role expectations among men and women characterizes the traditional American dating system.

Yes   No

6. Men and women generally agree on what constitutes a "consent" to have sex together.

Yes   No

7. Women know that when they request it, men will stop immediately during the sex act.

Yes   No

8. Attitudes toward members of the opposite sex are significant variables for predicting the tendency of an individual to rape.

Yes   No

9. It is all right for a male to force a female to engage in intercourse if she lets him touch her above the waist.

Yes   No

10. Women are more responsible than men for preventing date rape.

Yes   No

11. Men and women have difficulty expressing themselves honestly in new male/female relationships.

Yes   No

12. Forced sex is a crime even though the male and female may like each other or have had sex in the past.

Yes   No

13. It is never OK for a man to force himself on a woman even though he's heard the woman say "No" but he thinks she means "Yes."

Yes   No

14. A close look at American society strongly suggests that women and men are toys for play or are objects for conquer.

Yes   No

15. Frequently women and men fail to report rape because of fear of humiliation.

Yes   No

16. Traditional American dating styles characterize men as aggressors and women as resistors.

Yes   No

Correct answers:

1. 10%	2. Yes	3. Yes	4. No	5. Yes	
6. No	7. No	8. Yes	9. No	10. No	
11. Yes	12. Yes	13. Yes	14. Yes	15. Yes	16. Yes

The Anatomy of a Date Rape

Directions: Ask a participant to read the **SITUATION** given below. Ask the same or another participant to read each question that follows. Allow group participants to discuss each question. Compare answers from male and female participants.

SITUATION: It was Julie's first time away from home. It was her second date with Tom, another freshman student at College U. Both Julie and Tom had breakfast and dinner together in the campus dining center, walked to several classes together, and had study dates in the past. They had become friends! Tonight's party had been fun and gamely. Beer and wine were the only refreshments served; jokes centered on sexual activities; marijuana was smoked; everyone professed to have a good time.

After the party, Tom and Julie returned to Tom's dorm room where both began to become intimate with each other, engaging in petting and kissing. With time, Julie asked Tom to stop, but he persisted because Tom knew that Julie wanted it. Tom also knew that Julie was a tease! She protested but Tom continued and eventually coerced her into having sex with him. Tom returned Julie to her dorm room to end the evening.

Questions for Discussion:

1. Did rape occur?
2. The forced act of sex occurred on whose turf?
3. Identify factors that may have contributed to the forced act of sex.
4. What was Tom's perception of Julie? As a person? College student? Friend? Date?
5. What have you learned?

Sexual Assertiveness Questionnaire

Directions: Place the number in the blank that best indicates your response
to the statements below.

1 = Never

2 = Sometimes

3 = Always

People have the right to:

_____ 1. Make their own decisions regarding intercourse or other
sexual activity regardless of their partner's wishes.

_____ 2. Use or not use birth control regardless of their partner's
wishes.

_____ 3. Tell their partner when they want to make love.

_____ 4. Tell their partner they don't want to make love.

_____ 5. Tell their partner they won't have intercourse without birth
control.

_____ 6. Tell their partner they want to make love differently.

_____ 7. Masturbate to orgasm.

_____ 8. Tell their partner they are being too rough.

_____ 9. Tell their partner they want to be hugged or cuddled without sex.

_____ 10. Tell their relative they're uncomfortable being hugged or
kissed in certain ways.

_____ 11. Ask their partner if they have been examined for sexually
transmitted diseases.

Fishbowl Exercise

Directions: This exercise occurs with the women initially sitting in the
middle of a circle and the men on the outside. The group facilitator reads
each of the unfinished sentences stated below and the women respond
while the men listen. The process is then reversed. The men sit in the middle
of the circle and the women on the outside. The men respond to the
unfinished sentences while the women listen. Later, the group discusses
similarities and differences in the responses and implications of the responses for dating.

1. Situations in which I feel vulnerable are . . .

2. Cues that make me wary are . . .

3. I feel I have a right to sex when . . .

4. I feel someone is giving me a sexual "come on" when . . .

5. I feel powerless in a relationship when . . .

Date-Rape Workshop Evaluation Form

I. How effective was the workshop in helping you achieve the following goals:

	Very Ineffective		Uncertain		Very Effective
a. Increased awareness of the prevalence of date rape.	1	2	3	4	5
b. Increased awareness of the sociocultural forces contributing to date rape.	1	2	3	4	5
c. Helped me to be aware of how some of my own communication styles might contribute to a misunderstanding about sexual matters between me and the opposite sex.	1	2	3	4	5
d. Has helped me to better understand how to avoid a misunderstanding about sexual matters with another person.	1	2	3	4	5
e. Has given me a greater sense of responsibility in sexual situations.	1	2	3	4	5

II. How effective were the workshop leaders in these areas:

f. Helping you to achieve the workshop goals.	1	2	3	4	5
g. Helping you feel comfortable in participating in the workshop.	1	2	3	4	5
h. Handling this somewhat difficult topic.	1	2	3	4	5

III. What part of the workshop was most helpful?

IV. What part of the workshop was least helpful?

V. How could the workshop have been improved?

I would rate my overall experience in this workshop as positive.

Strongly Disagree		Uncertain		Strongly Agree
1	2	3	4	5

SOURCE: Permission to reprint this material from *Developmental Issues on Campus: Focus on Date Rape* has been granted by Diana Pace, Ph.D., Grand Valley State University, Allendale, Michigan.

References

Abbey, A. (1982). Sex differences in attributions for friendly behavior: Do males misperceive females' friendliness? *Journal of Personality and Social Psychology, 42*, 830-838.

Abbey, A., Cozzarelli, C., McLaughlin, K., & Harnish, R. (1987). The effects of clothing and dyad sex composition on perceptions of sexual intent: Do women and men evaluate these cues differently. *Journal of Applied Social Psychology, 17*, 108-126.

Abbey, A., & Melby, C. (1983). The effects of nonverbal cues on gender differences in perception of sexual intent. *Sex Roles, 9*, 179-193.

Adams, C., & Fay, J. (1984). *Nobody told me it was rape*. Santa Cruz, CA: E.T.R. Publishers.

A generalist perspective on social work practice. (1992). Unpublished manuscript, University of Kentucky, College of Social Work, Lexington.

American Psychiatric Association. (1987). *Diagnostic and statistical manual of mental disorders* (3rd ed., rev.). Washington, DC: Author.

Amick, A. E., & Calhoun, K. S. (1987). Resistance to sexual aggression: Personality, attitudinal, and situational factors. *Archives of Sexual Behavior, 16*, 153-163.

Amir, M. (1971). *Patterns in forcible rape*. Chicago: University of Chicago Press.

Augustine, R. I. (1991). Marriage: The safe haven for rapists. *Journal of Family Law, 29*, 559-591.

Baldwin, J., & Oliver, J. (1975). Epidemiology and family characteristics of severely-abused children. *British Journal of Social Medicine, 29*, 205-221.

Barnard, C. P. (1990). Alcoholism and sex abuse in the family: Incest and marital rape. *Journal of Chemical Dependency Treatment, 3*, 131-144.

Barshis, V. R. (1983). The question of marital rape. *Women's Studies International Forum, 6*, 383-393.

Bass, E., & Davis, L. (1988). *The courage to heal*. New York: Harper & Row.

193

194   INTIMATE BETRAYAL

Berkowitz, A. (1992). College men as perpetrators of acquaintance rape and sexual assault: A review of recent research. *Journal of American College Health, 40,* 175-180.

Bernard, J., Bernard, S., & Bernard, M. (1985). Courtship violence and sex-typing. *Family Relations, 34,* 573-576.

Bernard, M., & Bernard, J. (1983). Violent intimacy: The family as a model for love relationships. *Family Relations, 32,* 283-286.

Bessmer, S. (1976). *The laws of rape.* New York: Praeger.

Best, C., Dansky, B., & Kilpatrick, D. (1992). Medical students' attitudes about female rape victims. *Journal of Interpersonal Violence, 7,* 175-188.

Bidwell, L., & White, P. (1986). The family context of marital rape. *Journal of Family Violence, 1,* 277-287.

Black, D. (1970). The social organization of arrest. *Stanford Law Review, 23,* 1087-1111.

Blake-White, J., & Kline, M. (1985). Treating the dissociative process in adult victims of childhood incest. *Social Casework, 60,* 394-402.

Blume, S. (1990). *Secret survivors uncovering incest and its aftereffects in women.* New York: John Wiley.

Bogal-Allbritten, R., & Allbritten, W. (1990, August). *Date rape and courtship violence: A model prevention program.* Paper presented at the ninety-eighth annual convention of the American Psychological Association, Boston.

Bohmer, C. (1991). Acquaintance rape and the law. In A. Parrot & L. Bechofter (Eds.), *Acquaintance rape: The hidden crime* (pp. 317-333). New York: John Wiley.

Boulding, E. (1978). Women and social violence. *International Social Science Journal, 1,* 801-815.

Bridges, J. S., & McGrail, C. A. (1989). Attributions of responsibility for date and stranger rape. *Sex Roles, 21,* 273-286.

Brownmiller, S. (1975). *Against our will: Men, women and rape.* New York: Simon & Schuster.

Burgess, A., & Holmstrom, L. (1974). Rape trauma syndrome. *American Journal of Psychiatry, 131,* 981-986.

Burgess, A. W., & Holmstrom, L. L. (1979). *Rape crisis and recovery.* Bowie, MD: Robert J. Brady.

Burkhardt, B. (1991). Conceptual and practical analysis of therapy for acquaintance rape victims. In A. Parrot & L. Bechofter (Eds.), *Acquaintance rape: The hidden crime* (pp. 27-39). New York: John Wiley.

Burt, C. (1985). The crime of marital rape. *Family Advocate, 7,* 22-25.

Burt, M. (1983). Cultural myths and support for rape. *Journal of Personality and Social Psychology, 45,* 344-356.

Calhoun, K., & Townsley, R. (1991). Attributions of responsibility for acquaintance rape. In A. Parrot & L. Bechofter (Eds.), *Acquaintance rape: The hidden crime* (pp. 57-69). New York: John Wiley.

California Penal Code (Vol. 1, Sec. 261). (1991). St. Paul, MN: West.

Caringella-MacDonald, S. (1988). Parallels and pitfalls: The aftermath of legal reform for sexual assault, marital rape, and domestic violence victims. *Journal of Interpersonal Violence, 3,* 174-189.

Coleman, C. (1978). Sex and the law. *Humanist, 38,* 38-41.

Coller, S., & Resick, R. (1987). Women's attributions of responsibility for date rape: The influence of empathy and sex-role stereotyping. *Violence and Victims, 2,* 115-125.

Comfort, A. (1972). *The joy of sex.* New York: Crown.

Commonwealth v. Taylor, 338 Pa. Sup., 487 A.2d. 946 (1985).

Conger, R., Burgess, R., & Barrett, C. (1979). Child abuse related to life change and perceptions of illness: Some preliminary findings. *Family Coordinator, 58,* 73-77.

Corey, G., Corey, M. S., & Callanan, P. (1984). *Issues and ethics in the helping professions* (2nd ed.). Monterey, CA: Brooks/Cole.

Cournoyer, B. (1989, September). Self-understanding and self-discipline in social work practice. In "Clinically Speaking," a column of the *Indiana Chapter Newsletter.* (Available from Indiana Chapter National Association of Social Workers, 1100 W. 42nd St., Indianapolis, IN 46208)

Dolan, Y. M. (1991). *Resolving sexual abuse: Solution-focused therapy and Ericksonian hypnosis for adult survivors.* New York: W. W. Norton.

Dolan, Y. (1992). *Resolving sexual abuse.* New York: Free Press.

Dull, R. T., & Giacopassi, D. J. (1987). Demographic correlates of sexual and dating attitudes. *Criminal Justice and Behavior, 14,* 175-193.

Ehrhart, J. K., & Sandler, B. R. (1985). *Campus gang rape: Party games?* Washington, DC: Association of American Colleges.

Ellis, E. M., Atkeson, B. M., & Calhoun, K. S. (1981). An assessment of long-term reaction to rape. *Journal of Abnormal Psychology, 90,* 263-266.

Ellis, J., & "Eve." (1990). The therapeutic journey: A guide for travelers. In T. Laidlaw, C. Malmo, & Associates (Eds.), *Healing voices: Feminist approaches to therapy with women* (pp. 243-271). San Francisco: Jossey-Bass.

Ellis, L. (1989). *Theories of rape.* New York: Hemisphere.

Elmer, E. (1950). Abused children seen in hospitals. *Social Work, 5,* 98-102.

Estrich, S. (1987). *Real rape.* Cambridge, MA: Harvard University Press.

Falaler, K. (1989). Characteristics of a clinical sample of sexually abused children: How boy and girl victims differ. *Child Abuse & Neglect, 13,* 281-291.

Feild, H., & Bienen, L. (1980). *Jurors and rape: A study in psychology and law.* Lexington, MA: Lexington Books.

Fischer, G. J. (1986). College student attitudes toward forcible date rape: I. Cognitive predictors. *Archives of Sexual Behavior, 15,* 457-466.

Fortune, M. (1983). *Sexual violence: The unmentionable sin.* New York: Pilgrim.

Fortune, M. M. (1989). *Is nothing sacred? When sex invades the pastoral relationship.* San Francisco: Harper.

Foster, M. G. (1977). Eliminating sex discrimination in the law. *Social Casework, 58,* 67-76.

Frank, E., Turner, S. M., & Stewart, B. D. (1980). Initial response to rape: The impact of factors within the rape situation. *Journal of Behavioral Assessment, 2,* 39-53.

Freeman, M. D. (1985). Doing his best to sustain the sanctity of marriage. *Sociological Review Monograph, 31,* 124-146.

Frieze, I. H. (1983). Investigating the causes and consequences of marital rape. *Signs: Journal of Women in Culture and Society, 8,* 532-553.

Fromm, B. (1991). Sexual battery: Mixed-signal legislation reveals need for further reform. *Florida State University Law Review, 18,* 579-605.

Gelles, R. J. (1977). Power, sex, and violence: The case of marital rape. *Family Coordinator, 26,* 339-347.

Gidycz, C., & Koss, M. (1991). The effects of acquaintance rape on the female victim. In A. Parrot & L. Bechofter (Eds.), *Acquaintance rape: The hidden crime* (pp. 270-283). New York: John Wiley.

Gilbert, S. (1992). Ethical issues in the treatment of severe psychopathology in university and college counseling centers. *Journal of Counseling and Development, 70,* 695-699.

Gise, L., & Paddison, P. (1988). Rape, sexual abuse, and its victims. *Psychiatric Clinics of North America, 11,* 629-648.

Gondolf, E. W. (1985). Forum: Fighting for control: A clinical assessment of men who batter. *Social Casework, 66,* 48-54.

Green, A., Gaines, R., & Sandgrund, A. (1974). Child abuse: Pathological syndrome of family interaction. *American Journal of Psychiatry, 131,* 882-886.

Hale, M. (1991). *History of the pleas of the crown.* London: Professional Books. (Original work published in 1736)

Hall, E. (1987). Adolescents' perception of sexual assault. *Journal of Sex Education and Therapy, 13,* 37-42.

Hall, G. N., & Hirschman, R. (1991). Toward a theory of sexual aggression: A quadripartite model. *Journal of Consulting and Clinical Psychology, 59,* 662-669.

Hanneke, C. R., Shields, N. M., & McCall, G. J. (1986). Assessing the prevalence of marital rape. *Journal of Interpersonal Violence, 1,* 350-362.

Harman, J. D. (1984). Consent, harm, and marital rape. *University of Louisville School of Law, 22,* 423-443.

Harney, P. A., & Muelenhard, C. L. (1991). Factors that increase the likelihood of victimization in acquaintance rape. In A. Parrot & L. Bechofter (Eds.), *Acquaintance rape: The hidden crime* (pp. 159-175). New York: John Wiley.

Herman, J. L. (1992). *Trauma and recovery.* New York: Basic Books.

Herman, J., & Hirschman, L. (1977). Father-daughter incest. *Signs: Journal of Women in Culture and Society, 4,* 735-756.

Hollis, J. (1985). *Fat is a family affair.* New York: Harper/Hazelden.

Holmstrom, L. L., & Burgess, A. W. (1983). Rape and everyday life. *Society, 20,* 33-40;

Holtzman, E. (1986). Women and the law. *Villanova Law Review, 31,* 1429-1438.

Hughes, J. O., & Sandler, B. (1987, April). *"Friends" raping friends: Could it happen to you?* Project on the Status and Education of Women, Center for Women Policy Studies. (Available from the Center for Women Policy Studies, 2000 P Street, NW, Suite 508, Washington, DC 20036)

Issori, K., & Reubin, A. R. (1986). *Psychoeducational group manual.* (Available from the Assault Crisis Center, Washtenaw County Community Mental Health, Ann Arbor, MI 48106, 313/483-7942.)

Janoff-Bulman, R. (1992). *Shattered assumptions: Toward a new psychology of trauma.* New York: Free Press.

Jeffords, C. R. (1984). The impact of sex-role and religious attitudes upon forced marital intercourse norms. *Sex Roles, 11,* 543-552.

Jeffords, C. R., & Dull, R. T. (1982). Demographic variations in attitudes towards marital rape immunity. *Journal of Marriage and the Family, 44,* 755-762.

Jenkins, M., & Dambrot, F. (1987). The attribution of date rape: Observer's attitudes and sexual experiences and the dating situation. *Journal of Applied Social Psychology, 17,* 875-895.

Johnson, A. G. (1980). On the prevalence of rape in the United States. *Signs: Journal of Women in Culture and Society, 6,* 136-146.

Johnson, B., & Morse, H. (1968). Injured children and their parents. *Children, 15,* 147-152.

Johnson, D., & VanVonderen, J. (1991). *The subtle power of spiritual abuse.* Minneapolis, MN: Bethany House.

Johnson, S. A. (1992). *Man-to-man: When your partner says "no."* Orwell, VT: Safer Society Press.

Johnson v. State, 598 Aq. 2d 5 (Tenn. Crim. 1979).

Kaminer, W. (1993, October). Feminism's identity crisis. *Atlantic Monthly, 272,* 51-68.

Katz, B. (1991). The psychological impact of stranger versus nonstranger rape on victims' recovery. In A. Parrot & L. Bechofter (Eds.), *Acquaintance rape: The hidden crime* (pp. 251-269). New York: John Wiley.

Kaufman, J., & Zigler, E. (1987). Do abused children become abusive parents? *American Journal of Orthopsychiatry, 57,* 186-192.

Kerstetter, W. A. (1990). Gateway to justice: Police and prosecutorial response to sexual assaults against women. *Journal of Criminal Law and Criminology, 81,* 267-313.

Kerstetter, W. A., & Van Winkle, B. (1990). Who decides? A study of the complainant's decision to prosecute in rape cases. *Criminal Justice and Behavior, 17,* 268-283.

Kilpatrick, D. G., Best, C. L., Saunder, B. E., & Veronen, L. V. (1988). Rape in marriage and in dating relationships: How bad is it for mental health? *Annals of the New York Academy of Science, 528,* 335-344.

Kilpatrick, D. G., Veronen, L. J., & Best, C. L. (1985). Factors predicting psychological distress among rape victims. In C. R. Figley (Ed.), *Trauma and its wake: The study and treatment of post-traumatic stress disorder* (pp. 113-141). New York: Brunner/Mazel.

King, M. (Ed.). (1992). *Male victims of sexual assault.* Oxford: Oxford University Press.

Koss, M. (1985). The hidden rape victim: Personality, attitudinal, and situational characteristics. *Psychology of Women Quarterly, 9,* 193-212.

Koss, M., & Burkhardt, B. (1989). A conceptual analysis of rape victimization long term effects and implications for treatment. *Psychology of Women Quarterly, 13,* 27-39.

Koss, M. P., Dinero, T. E., Seibel, C. A., & Cox, S. L. (1988). Stranger and acquaintance rape: Are there differences in the victim's experience? *Psychology of Women Quarterly, 12,* 1-24.

Koss, M., Gidycz, C., & Wisniewski, N. (1987). The scope of rape: Incidence and prevalence of sexual aggression and victimization a national sample of higher education students. *Journal of Consulting and Clinical Psychology, 55,* 162-170.

Kottler, J. (1986). *On being a therapist.* San Francisco: Jossey-Bass.

Laidlaw, T. A., Malmo, C., & Associates. (1990). *Healing voices: Feminist approaches to therapy with women.* San Francisco: Jossey-Bass.

Laidlaw, T. A., & "Michaela." (1990). In E. Laidlaw, C. Malmo, & Associates (Eds.), *Healing voices: Feminist approaches to therapy with women* (pp. 15-32). San Francisco: Jossey-Bass.

Ledray, L. (1986). *Recovery from rape.* New York: Henry Holt.

Lerner, H. G. (1985). *The dance of anger.* New York: Harper & Row.

Loggans, S. (1985). Rape as an intentional tort: First- and third-party liability. *Trial, 21,* 45-55.

Lopez, P. (1992). He said . . . She said . . . : An overview of date rape from commission through prosecution through verdict. *Criminal Justice Journal, 13,* 275-302.

Mackinnon, C. A. (1983). Feminism, Marxism, method, and the state: Toward feminist jurisprudence. *Signs: Journal of Women in Culture and Society, 8,* 635-658.

Margolin, L., Miller, M., & Moran, P. (1989). When a kiss is not just a kiss: Relating violations of consent in kissing to rape myth acceptance. *Sex Roles, 20,* 231-243.

Marhoefer-Dvorak, S. A., Resick, P. A., Hutter, C. K., & Girelli, S. A. (1988). Single-versus multiple-incident rape victims: A comparison of psychological reactions to rape. *Journal of Interpersonal Violence, 3,* 145-160.

Marsh, J., Geist, J., & Caplan, N. (1987). *Rape and the limits of law reform.* Boston: Auburn House.

McGuire, L., & Wagner, N. (1978). Sexual dysfunction in women who were molested as children: One response pattern and suggestions for treatment. *Journal of Sex and Marital Therapy, 1,* 11-15.

McLaughlin, M. (1991). Rape trauma syndrome. In *American jurisprudence, proof of facts* (3rd ser., Vol. 12, pp. 401-503). Rochester, NY: Lawyers Cooperative.

Miller, B. (1988). Date rape: Time for a new look at prevention. *Journal of College Student Development, 29,* 553-555.

Milne, A., Salem, P., & Koeffler, K. (1992). When domestic abuse is an issue. *Family Advocate, 14,* 34-39.

Muehlenhard, C. (1987). Date rape and sexual aggression in dating situations: Incidence and risk factors. *Journal of Counseling Psychology, 34,* 186-196.

Muehlenhard, C. L. (1988). Misinterpreted dating behaviors and the risk of date rape. *Journal of Social and Clinical Psychology, 6,* 29-37.

Muehlenhard, C. L., Friedman, D. E., & Thomas, C. M. (1985). Is date rape justifiable? *Psychology of Women Quarterly, 9,* 297-310.

Muehlenhard, C. L., & Linton, M. A. (1987). Date rape and sexual aggression in dating situations: Incidence and risk factors. *Journal of Counseling Psychology, 34,* 186-196.

Nurse, S. (1964). Familial patterns of parents who abuse their children. *Smith College Studies, 35,* 11-25.

Oliver, J., & Taylor, A. (1971). Five generations of ill-treated children in one family pedigree. *British Journal of Psychiatry, 119,* 473-480.

Pagelow, M. D. (1992). Adult victims of domestic violence: Battered women. *Journal of Interpersonal Violence, 7,* 87-120.

Parrot, A. (1988a). *Coping with date rape & acquaintance rape.* New York: Rosen.

Parrot, A. (1988b). *Date rape and acquaintance rape.* New York: Rosen.

Parrot, A. (1991). Medical community response to acquaintance rape—Recommendations. In A. Parrot & L. Bechofter (Eds.), *Acquaintance rape: The hidden crime* (pp. 304-316). New York: John Wiley.

Patten, S., Gatz, Y., Jones, B., & Thomas, D. (1989). Posttraumatic stress disorder and the treatment of sexual abuse. *Social Work, 34,* 197-203.

Paulson, M. J., & Chaleff, A. (1973). Parent surrogate roles: A dynamic concept in understanding and treating abusive parents. *Journal of Clinical and Consulting Child Psychology, 2,* 38-40.

People v. Varon, 143 Ca. App. 3d 566, 192 Ca. Rep. 44 (1983, 2d Dist.).

Pfeiffer, M. (1990). Date rape: The reality. *Southern University Law Review, 17,* 283-295.

Pineau, L. (1989). Date rape: A feminist analysis. *Law & Philosophy, 8,* 217-243.

Police discretion and the judgment that a crime has been committed: Rape in Philadelphia [Comment]. (1968). *University of Pennsylvania Law Review, 117,* 277-292.

Ramsey-Klawsnik, H. (1991). Elder sexual abuse: Preliminary findings. *Journal of Elder Abuse and Neglect, 3,* 73-90.

The rape shield paradox: Complainant protection amidst oscillating trends of judicial interpretation [Comment]. (1987). *Journal of Criminal Law and Criminology, 78,* 644-698.

Rapport, K. R., & Posey, C. D. (1991). Sexually coercive college males. In A. Parrot & L. Bechofter (Eds.), *Acquaintance rape: The hidden crime* (pp. 217-228). New York: John Wiley.

Richardson, D. R., & Hammock, G. S. (1991). Alcohol and acquaintance rape. In A. Parrot & L. Bechofter (Eds.), *Acquaintance rape: The hidden crime* (pp. 83-95). New York: John Wiley.

Ruch, M. L. O., & Chandler, S. M. (1983). Sexual assault trauma during the acute phase: An exploratory model and multivariate analysis. *Journal of Health and Social Behavior, 24,* 174-185.

Russell, D. (1975). *The politics of rape.* New York: Stein & Day.

Russell, D. E. H. (1982). *Rape in marriage.* New York: Macmillan.

Russell, D. E. H. (1986). *The secret trauma: Incest in the lives of girls and women.* New York: Basic Books.

Russell, D. (1991). Wife rape. In A. Parrot & L. Bechofer (Eds.), *Acquaintance rape: The hidden crime* (pp. 129-139). New York: John Wiley.

Schaef, A. W. (1986). *Co-dependence misunderstood-mistreated.* San Francisco: Harper & Row.

Schaef, A. W. (1992). *Beyond therapy, beyond science* (Audiocassettes). New York: HarperCollins.

Scheyett, A. (1988). Marriage is the best defense: Policy on marital rape. *Affilia: Journal of Women and Social Work, 3,* 8-23.

Selkin, J. (1979). Protecting personal space: Victim and resister reactions to assaultive rape. *Journal of Community Psychology, 6,* 263-268.

Shotland, L., & Goldstein, L. (1983). Just because she doesn't want to doesn't mean it's rape: An experimentally based causal model of the perception of rape in a dating situation. *Social Psychology Quarterly, 446,* 220-232.

Silver, L., Dublin, C., & Lourie, R. (1969). Does violence breed violence? Contributions from a study of the child abuse syndrome. *American Journal of Psychiatry, 126,* 404-407.

Small, M. A., & Tetreault, P. A. (1990). Social psychology, "marital rape exemptions," and privacy. *Behavioral Sciences and the Law, 8,* 141-149.

Smith, J., & Williams, J. (1992). From abusive household to dating violence. *Journal of Family Violence, 7,* 153-165.

State v. Romer, App. 94 NM 22, 606 P.2d, 1116 (1980).

State v. Snow, 252 Aq. 629 (Mo. 1923).

Strean, H. (1985). *Therapeutic principles in social work practice.* Northvale, NJ: Jason Aronson.

Struckman-Johnson, C. (1991). Male victims of acquaintance rape. In A. Parrot & L. Bechofter (Eds.), *Acquaintance rape: The hidden crime* (pp. 192-213). New York: John Wiley.

Sullivan, J. P., & Mosher, D. L. (1990). Acceptance of guided imagery of marital rape as a function of macho personality. *Violence and Victims, 5,* 275-286.

Summit, R., & Kryso, J. (1978). Sexual abuse of children: A clinical spectrum. *Clinical Social Work Journal, 1,* 62-77.

Tasi, M., Feldman-Summers, S., & Edgar, M. (1979). Childhood molestation: Variables related to differential impacts on psychosexual functioning in adult women. *Journal of Abnormal Psychology, 88,* 407-417.

Taylor, J. (1987). Rape and women's credibility: Problems of recantations and false accusations in the case of Cathleen Crowell Webb and Gary Dodson. *Harvard Women's Law Journal, 10,* 59-116.

Troop, N. (1992, October). *Looking forward to the future: New ideas about rape.* Paper presented at the Woman's Conference, University of Kentucky, Lexington.

U.S. Department of Justice. (1991). *Female victims of violent crime.* (Special Report NCJ-126826). Washington, DC: Government Printing Office.

Walker, L. (1984). *The battered woman syndrome.* New York: Springer.

Warshaw, R. (1988). *I never called it rape.* New York: Harper & Row.

Wiehe, V. (1990). *Sibling abuse: The hidden physical, emotional, and sexual trauma.* New York: Lexington.

Wiehe, V. (1992). Abusive and nonabusive parents: How they were parented. *Journal of Social Service Research, 15,* 81-93.

Wiener, R. (1983). Shifting the communication burden: A meaningful consent standard in rape. *Harvard Women's Law Journal, 6,* 143-161.

Wigmore, J. (1971). *Evidence* (Chadbourn rev., 3A Sec. 924a). St. Paul, MN: West.

Williams, K. (1981). Few convictions in rape cases: Empirical evidence concerning some alternative explanations. *Journal of Criminal Justice, 9,* 29-39.

Yegidis, B. L. (1988). Wife abuse and marital rape among women who seek help. *Affilia: Journal of Women and Social Work, 3,* 62-68.

Index

About the Authors

Gary W. Paquin, JD, PhD, is an Assistant Professor in the College of Social Work at the University of Kentucky at Lexington. He received his master's and law degrees from the University of Michigan and his doctorate from the University of California, Berkeley. He is a member of the California Bar Association. He conducts research and writes in the areas of conflict resolution and legal/social work issues.

Patricia Lynn Peacock, MSW, CSW received her Bachelor of Arts degree from Meredith College in Raleigh, North Carolina, and her Master of Social Work degree from the University of Kentucky at Lexington. She is currently working on her doctorate in social work at the University of Tennessee at Knoxville, where she is also a teaching assistant. In addition to her academic pursuits, she is employed as the social worker at the Pain Management Center at the University of Kentucky hospital. She has made presentations at both regional and national conferences.

Ann L. Richards, MSW, LCSW, received her Bachelor of Science degree from Northern Kentucky University in Highland Heights, Kentucky, and her Master of Social Work degree from the University of Kentucky at Lexington. She currently is employed as a clinical social worker at the Health, Counseling, and Testing Center at Northern Kentucky University and has also served as a part-time instructor at the university. Prior to this, she was the Associate Director of the Women's Crisis Center of Northern Kentucky at Covington, Kentucky. In addition to her professional employment, she is actively involved in a volunteer capacity with organizations working in the field of interpersonal violence. She is a past appointee by the Governor of Kentucky to the Kentucky Child Abuse and Exploitation Prevention Board. She has made presentations at local, regional, and national conferences.

Vernon R. Wiehe, PhD, is Professor in the College of Social Work at the University of Kentucky at Lexington. After he received a master's degree from the University of Chicago, he did postgraduate work in the Program of Advanced Studies in Social Work at Smith College. He received his doctorate from Washington University in St. Louis. He is the author of numerous articles in professional journals as well as the following books: *Sibling Abuse: The Hidden Physical, Emotional, and Sexual Trauma; Perilous Rivalry: When Siblings Become Abusive; Working With Child Abuse and Neglect;* and *Uncovering Sibling Abuse.* He has appeared on numerous television and radio talk shows discussing family violence, including the *Donahue Show* and *Sonya Live.* He is a frequently cited author on the subject of family violence.